ANOINTED
TRANSFORMED
REDEEMED
A Study of David

PRISCILLA SHIRER
BETH MOORE
KAY ARTHUR

LifeWay Press®
Nashville, Tennessee

Published by LifeWay Press®
© 2008 • LifeWay Christian Resources
Sixth printing May 2011

No part of this book may be reproduced or transmitted in any form or
by any means, electronic or mechanical, including photocopying and recording,
or by any information storage or retrieval system, except as may be expressly
permitted in writing by the publisher. Requests for permission should be addressed
in writing to LifeWay Press®; One LifeWay Plaza; Nashville, TN 37234-0175.

ISBN 9781415865859
Item 005159143

Dewey Decimal Classification Number: 248.84
Subject Heading: DAVID. KING OF ISRAEL \ CHRISTIAN LIFE \ BIBLE STUDY

Scripture quotations marked NIV are from the Holy Bible, New International Version
Copyright © 1973, 1978, 1984 by International Bible Society. Scripture quotations
marked HCSB® are taken from the Holman Christian Standard Bible®, copyright
© 1999, 2000, 2002, 2003 by Holman Bible Publishers. Used by permission.
Scripture quotations marked NASB are taken from the New American Standard
Bible®, Copyright 1960, 1962, 1963, 1968, 1971, 1972, 1973, 1975, 1977, 1995
by The Lockman Foundation. Used by permission. (www.lockman.org) References
taken from The NEW LIFE Testament are identified (N.L.T.). It is published by the
Christian Literature International, Canby, Oregon, and is used by permission. Scripture
quotations marked The Message are from THE MESSAGE, © 1993, 1994, 1995, 1996.
Used by permission of NavPress Publishing Group. Scripture quotations marked
NET are from The Net Bible®. New English Translation Copyright © 1996 by Biblical
Studies Press, L.L.C. Net Bible® is a registered trandemark. The Net Bible® logo,
service mark copyright © 1997 by Biblical Studies Press, L.L.C.
All rights reserved.

To order additional copies of this resource:
Write LifeWay Church Resources Customer Service;
One LifeWay Plaza; Nashville, TN 37234-0113;
fax order to (615) 251-5933; call toll free 1-800-458-2772;
e-mail orderentry@lifeway.com; order online at www.lifeway.com;
or visit the LifeWay Christian Store serving you.

Printed in the United States of America

Leadership and Adult Publishing
LifeWay Church Resources
One LifeWay Plaza
Nashville, Tennessee 37234-0175

Contents

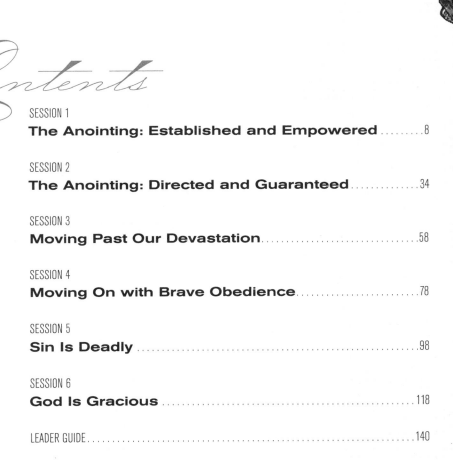

Introduction

These three women, representing three generations committed to God and His Word, have been a huge blessing to millions. When they worked with LifeWay to do the Deeper Still events, we knew God was doing something special. So some of the team members in women's ministry began to dream. *What if we videotaped a Deeper Still conference so many more women could share the experience?* Then the vision began to grow. *What if we got each of these Bible study teachers to write two weeks material to go along with what they taught at the event?*

Those of us who had seen Kay, Beth, and Priscilla teach on David agreed that such a resource would do several things.
* It would give students a chance to get to know these three Bible teachers.
* It would reinforce the message these three have been emphasizing for years—that we should never follow one teacher, but we should diversify our spiritual portfolio by learning from many of God's leaders.
* It would be an outstanding look at the life of King David from three perspectives.
* And it would be just the kind of shorter-duration study that many ministry leaders have been requesting.

Then came the obstacle. These three women are incredibly busy in ministry. Overcommitted. Swamped. We'd feel reticent to even ask them to take on another project, but in a conversation with Priscilla, we suggested the idea. In true Texas-girl fashion, Priscilla took the bull by the horns. She said she'd get Beth and Kay to agree. Some talk of twisting arms might have been included in the conversation.

So thanks Priscilla for twisting arms. And welcome Bible students to what was going to be called the *Deeper Still Bible Study*. Because of a title conflict we sought an alternate name, and then we realized God led Priscilla to teach on David's anointing and ours. God led Beth to transformation. And Kay tied it all up with a bow teaching on redemption as the mark of God's children. Thus was born *Anointed, Transformed, Redeemed: A Study of David*.

Meet the three amazing women who will be our leaders for the next six sessions:

ABOUT THE
AUTHORS

BETHMOORE

PRISCILLASHIRER

KAYARTHUR

Priscilla Shirer is a Bible teacher whose ministry is focused on the expository teaching of the Word of God to women. Her desire is to see women not only know the uncompromising truths of Scripture intellectually but experience them practically by the power of the Holy Spirit. Priscilla is a graduate of the Dallas Theological Seminary with a Master's degree in Biblical Studies. For over a decade she has been a conference speaker for major corporations, organizations, and Christian audiences across the United States and the world.

Priscilla is now in full-time ministry to women. She is the author of *A Jewel in His Crown, A Jewel in His Crown Journal, And We Are Changed: Transforming Encounters with God, He Speaks to Me: Preparing to Hear from God, Discerning the Voice of God: How to Recognize When God Speaks,* and *Can We Talk? Soul-Stirring Conversations with God.* Priscilla is the daughter of pastor, speaker, and well-known author Dr. Tony Evans. She is married to her best friend, Jerry. The couple resides in Dallas with their two young sons, Jackson and Jerry Jr. Jerry and Priscilla have founded Going Beyond Ministries, where they are committed to seeing believers receive the most out of their relationships with the Lord.

ABOUT THE
AUTHORS

Beth Moore has written best-selling Bible studies on David, Moses, Paul, Isaiah, Daniel, John, and Jesus. Her books *Breaking Free, Praying God's Word,* and *When Godly People Do Ungodly Things* have all focused on the battle Satan is waging against Christians. *Believing God, Loving Well,* and *Living Beyond Yourself* have focused on how Christians can live triumphantly in today's world. In *Stepping Up* Beth leads Christians to reach a new level of relationship and intimacy with God. Beth has a passion for Christ, a passion for Bible study, and a passion to see Christians living the lives Christ intended.

Beth is an active member of First Baptist Church of Houston, Texas. The wife of Keith, mother of two young adult daughters Melissa and Amanda, and grandmother of Jackson, Beth serves a worldwide audience through Living Proof Ministry. Her conference ministry, writing, and videos reach millions of people every year.

Kay Arthur In the late 1960s a missionary couple in Mexico suffered medical problems and returned home to Chattanooga, Tennessee. Little did they know that God had a greater field of ministry for them. Jack Arthur became station manager for a Christian radio station, and Kay Arthur started a Bible study for teenagers in their living room. By 1970 youth were meeting in a barn they had cleaned out and patched up themselves. Soon adults were coming too.

The first women's Bible study class began, and the word spread. Nights classes started. Soon Kay was traveling to Atlanta, Georgia, every week to teach nearly 1,800 adults. Knowing she and Jack would not be able to travel every week, Kay wanted to teach others to study inductively and so began writing Precept Upon Precept courses.

Jack left his radio career and became president and leader of this flourishing new organization. Today Precept Ministries International (*www.precept.org*) reaches into 150 countries with studies in 70 languages for children, teens, and adults.

Through the many ministries of Precept—including the daily radio and television program "Precepts for Life," Kay Arthur had touched millions of lives. A well-known conference speaker and author, Kay has a unique ability to reach people in an exciting, effective way—teaching them how to discover truth for themselves so truth can change their lives and equip them to be used to advance God's kingdom.

PRISCILLA SHIRER

ANOINTED

SESSION 1

VIEWERGUIDE

THE ANOINTING: ESTABLISHED AND EMPOWERED

1. First Chronicles 14:2 tells us that David knew two things: He knew _____ he was, and he knew _____ he was.

2. The word "_____" is the same word used in Psalm 119:90 to talk about how the Lord established the earth or founded the earth.

3. When the Philistines heard that David had been _____ (1 Chron. 14:8).

4. The anointing is "a divine _____ or a divine _____ to accomplish God's purposes for your life."

5. If you are a believer in Jesus Christ, the _____ of God rests on your life.

6. The anointing guarantees _____.

7. David's first mission as king was to bring back the ark of God, which represented the _____ of God.

8. Personally bringing back the ark of God means setting up the presence of God as the _____ _____ _____ of every decision you make.

GROUP DISCUSSION QUESTIONS

1. David wanted the ark to be in Jerusalem as a symbol of God's presence. What represents God's presence to you?

2. What opposition did David face? What opposition do women who are trying to serve God face today?

WEEK ONE | DAY ONE
HANDPICKED BY GOD

"I have found David son of Jessie a man after my own heart" (Acts 13:22, NIV).

Nicole has been my sister-friend for over 20 years. She's a vivacious, beautiful, and godly 30-something and a delightful blessing in my life; but she has experienced much sadness and frustration. From her earliest childhood Nicole felt rejected by those she most hoped would love her. She never knew her father, and her fiancé called off their wedding. During each of those times, as she grappled with intense feelings of abandonment, the sweet words of Christ spoke to the depths of her wounded soul. His healing balm of love and grace poured on her as she read:

"You did not choose Me, but I chose you" (John 15:16, HCSB).

Choose comes from the Greek *eklegomai* meaning *to choose* and *out from*. Thus the compound word means *to pick, single out, to choose out*. The genius of the word has in it the idea of not merely choosing, but that of choosing out from a number. The elect are *the chosen-out ones*.[1]

Chosen ricocheted off of the hollow walls of Nicole's heart and invited her to rejoice in the love that led the King of the universe to hand select her. She turned her attention away from those who rejected her and refocused on the One who called her to Himself for His purposes. Knowing you've been handpicked can stunningly deepen your affection for the One who picked you.

God chose you! Let that sink in. ... GOD chose you. You may have been turned down by your boss, rejected by your spouse, ignored by your parents, looked over by your friends, or refused by your children; but you can rest in the loving arms of God. He tore Himself away from heaven to come and be with you—the one He loves and chose to be His own to accomplish His purposes in this generation.

1. **Do you most often feel:**
   * **Chosen by God**   or   * **Rejected by God?**
   * **Ignored by God**   or   * **Disciplined by God?**
   * **Loved by God**   or   * **Unloved by God?**

2. **What about your life makes you feel this way?**

Regardless of how you answered that question, take a moment to contemplate and rejoice in the truth of John 15:16.

3. How might knowing you've been hand selected by God deepen your affection for Him and affect your life decisions?

In the margin write the initials of people who have most rejected you. As you consider God's choosing you, mark through each set of initials, releasing them from the responsibility to make you feel wanted and needed. Now soak in the words of John 15:16 just as my friend Nicole did, and consider how this deepens your love and commitment to please God and not others.

ELECTED AGAINST ALL ODDS

The much-debated theological principle that illustrates our standing with God is election. If you are a believer, you are one of the elect. Election means simply to choose. It designates the glorious fact that God chooses us, so our confidence rests not in our faithfulness but in His. God grants favor and abundant blessing to His chosen as He allows them to participate in His purposes in this generation.

4. Read Ephesians 1:4-5; 1 Peter 1:1-2; and Colossians 3:12. Then underline the phrases that illustrate the principle of election. Scripture reveals that God elects us to:

Salvation   Specific Callings   Specific Tasks

I admit I've pondered election and questioned its fairness. While complete clarity in this matter may always be a hidden secret in the heart of God, I've still wondered: *How could a good God choose some and not others?* A simple illustration has helped me grapple with my questions.

Imagine that I offered a room full of people a free soft drink. For various reasons they each refused to accept, but instead of leaving I then pulled 20 aside from the crowd of 100 to a small room for a more intentional invitation. I told these 20 what it cost me to get these drinks for them. I made clear how important it would be to me if they would accept it. Would I have been unfair to the other 80? No. I offered all 100 the same thing while giving the 20 a more deliberate opportunity to share in the free blessing I have for them.

Remember the teaching of 1 Peter 1:2—God's foreknowledge is part of election. We absolutely cannot think that we control God's sovereign choices, but part of the reason God chooses who He does is because He knows the end from the beginning.

How do we deal with those we love who are not yet saved? How do we know if they are among the elect? We don't. So we pray for the Spirit to work, and we work to tell them about the love of Jesus. All the while we can be secure that God will take the initiative to work in people's hearts. This relieves any pressure for us to "save" people because we know God is in ultimate control.

5. Write the names of the people who you're praying will come to know the Lord.

"It is because of him that you are in Christ Jesus" (1 Cor. 1:30, NIV).

PICKED FOR A PURPOSE

Our six-week study of David, one of the most beloved persons in the entire Bible, could not begin in a more appropriate place. He had been chosen—elected by God—not only to be in relationship with Him but also to lead His chosen people Israel.

6. **Acts 13:22 reveals why God selected David to accomplish His purposes. Write this reason in your own words:**

7. **Choose two of the following passages as a resource and record some characteristics they reveal about the kind of person David was and the type of heart he had.**
   Psalm 78:71-72
   Psalm 51:1-4,10-13
   1 Samuel 22:1-2
   1 Samuel 17:44-45
   1 Samuel 24:1-22
   2 Samuel 2:4-7

God is still looking for men and women whose hearts will reflect His passions. He has a divine search party going. He is seeking "to show Himself strong for those whose hearts are completely His" (2 Chron. 16:9, HCSB). I sure want to see God in my everyday living, don't you? Turns out He desires to show up in my everyday living—in yours too. He desires and delights to make Himself known, but He desires first to find someone in whom He sees a holy boldness by His Spirit to live fully committed and passionately for Him like David did.

The public anointing of David as King of Israel was the outcome of what had taken place in private between David and God long before. David was anointed for his great service and his ministry as Israel's king because God, who discerns the hearts of all men, knew that David's heart was different from others. He had a prepared heart. We can learn much from how David's heart became prepared to so attract God's attention. Author Alan Redpath suggests that a simple look at Psalm 23 gives ample insight into David's heart. Let's look at each selected phrase and carefully consider what we find.

8. **What does each capitalized portion of Psalm 23 reveal about what David believed about God or what characterized David's lifestyle?**

¹The Lord is my shepherd; I SHALL NOT WANT

²He maketh me to LIE DOWN in green pastures: he leadeth me beside the STILL WATERS

³He leadeth me in the paths of RIGHTEOUSNESS

*⁴Thou preparest a table before me in the presence of my enemies …
MY CUP [OF THANKSGIVING] runneth over*

⁵Surely goodness and mercy shall follow me all the days of my life: AND I WILL DWELL IN THE HOUSE OF THE LORD FOREVER

David's writing shows a man who trusted God, led a life of quiet devotion, pursued holiness (despite his imperfection), was thankful, and remained consistently devoted to God regardless of life's circumstances.

9. How would you describe yourself in each of these areas?

Trust God	Rarely	Sometimes	When It's Convenient	Most Often
Prioritize Intimate Times of Quiet with God	Never	Sometimes	When It's Convenient	Often
Pursue Holy Living	Never	Sometimes	When It's Convenient	I'm Not Perfect But Holiness Is My Life Goal
Grateful	Never	Sometimes	When It's Convenient	Most Often

10. What is one specific thing you can do this week in each area to begin to develop a life characterized by these things?

The good news for all of us is that David wasn't born with a supernatural ability to do these things better than everyone else. He recognized that he was nothing more than a mere man shaped in iniquity and conceived in sin (Ps. 51:5, KJV). He, just like you and me, had sin as a legacy and needed the redemption of God's grace extended to him. So any good thing God saw in David's heart was only there as a result of David's response to God's work in him. God's electing us for His specific purposes rests on how we respond to His love and work in us by His Spirit.

Over the next six weeks I believe passionately that the Spirit of the living God will speak to you clearly. (How can He not when you are listening to and reading the likes of Miss Beth and Miss Kay!) You have not happened on this study by chance. You're here for Him to do a work in you. You must choose to respond so your heart might capture the attention of God like David's did. It doesn't matter what your past was like or even what you think now disqualifies you from God's plans. He has chosen you. You are handpicked by the Father. Now I urge you to "walk in a manner worthy of the calling with which you have been called" (Eph. 4:1, NASB).

11. Write a prayer to God. If you are a believer, thank Him for your status as one of His chosen ones. Ask Him to use this study to reshape your heart. Ask Him to soften your heart to listen, receive, and obey His Word.

WEEK ONE | DAY TWO
Centered On God

In our video session we looked at a story in the life of David. For the next two weeks we will study some of the principles from the sessions so we can flesh them out and apply them to our lives. As we consider what it means to be handpicked into God's family and for His purpose, let's begin by looking at our main Scripture verse from the session: 1 Chronicles 14:2. This one verse contains so much that we'll spend the rest of the week unpacking it.

"And David realized that the Lord had established him as king over Israel, and that his kingdom was highly exalted for the sake of His people Israel" (1 Chron. 14:2, NASB).

1. Answer the following questions:
   What did David realize?

   To whom did David attribute this?

   For what purpose did David realize that this had been done?

Consider the following time line of David's life. Scholars debate some of the exact years, but it gives an accurate overview of David's life.[2] Note the date He was anointed king by the prophet Samuel, the date he defeated Goliath, the date he became king over the southern portion of Israel and the date he began his rule over all of Israel.

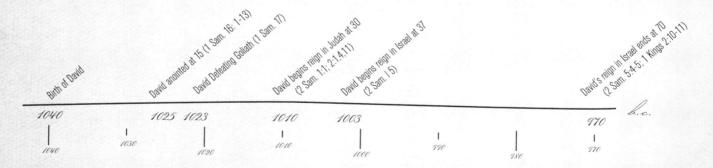

David was 37 years old when he began his reign over all Israel. Samuel had anointed him for the task 22 years earlier. Now as David finally sat on the throne, he realized God had given him this position. David knew that God was the source of his station in life as well as the station to which God's people had been called. No other explanation fit other than God.

2. Consider the following verses regarding each pivotal stage in David's life. How could David clearly see God's presence at each time?

Divine favor at his anointing—1 Samuel 16:7-13

Divine courage in defeating Goliath—1 Samuel 17:34-37

Divine timing in becoming king over Judah—2 Samuel 2:1-4

Divine authorization to be king over Israel—1 Chronicles 11:1-3

3. List four pivotal times in your life. How can you recognize the thread of God's presence with you during those times?

1.

2.

3.

4.

God's hand clearly has guided many circumstances in my life. I see many of these looking back. His hand appeared during joyful times but even more in painful circumstances. As a heartbroken, lovesick college student, I mourned the loss of a relationship I was certain would lead to marriage. After years of dating and courtship, I'd already mentally and emotionally bought the dress, picked the bridesmaids, and walked down the aisle. When it became obvious the relationship would end, I was devastated. I slid into a depression that threatened my mental and physical health. When I resurfaced, I came face-to-face with God's man for me—Jerry Shirer.

Now, 10 years later, I thank God more than anything for unanswered prayer. If He had given me what I was begging Him for at the time, I most likely would not be in ministry and certainly not alongside my spouse. God knew what He had in store for my life, and although it took a painful experience to steer me onto His path, I clearly see His hand guiding me, and I recognize His purposes amid that time of hurt. Remembering God's activity enables me to more fully trust His involvement in my circumstances now.

4. What did you learn about God in the four life circumstances you listed?

5. How does this assist you in trusting God more fully in your current life situations?

A "GOD-CONSCIOUSNESS"

Taking time to look back over the triumphs and devastations of our lives to find God's activity forms a worthwhile pastime. When we see that God has been with us all along, guiding our steps and directing our paths, we come to more fully trust Him and turn our attention to find Him more quickly in each new phase life brings. David, recognizing God's hand in his life, made a pivotal decision at the beginning of his reign over God's people.

6. According to 1 Chronicles 13:2-4, what was David's priority and desire as the new king?

The ark represented God among His people. For centuries this sacred chest not only symbolized but evidenced God's presence. God promised to meet with and speak to His children there (Ex. 25:22). No doubt years of personal communion with God had seared into David's mind the need for such divine meetings. He knew it would be impossible to rule with power and for Israel to remain separated from other people groups without the indwelling of and communion with God.

In David's mind, before any other kingdom work could be accomplished, the ark of God had to come back to its rightful position in Jerusalem. The shekinah glory of God with His people was David's concern, and bringing the ark back was not just his desire, it was his practical priority. Neglected by Saul and stolen during a time of war by the Philistines, the ark had been out of its rightful place for nearly 70 years. Now David decided it was time to bring back God's presence.

The mantra of David's life as a shepherd boy and as a king was the same "Let's bring back the ark of God to us."

7. Why do you think mere knowledge of God's presence with the people would not suffice for David?

8. Why would David want the physical demonstration of God's presence?

David's goal was to return the ark to the epicenter of the nation. Jerusalem was to be the social, economic, and spiritual center of the nation. David wanted God's presence and perspective to guide that center. He didn't want God's input to be separated from the practical rhythms of the people's lives but for God's people to live each day with a God-consciousness—an awareness of His presence with them.

Consider the record of David's first attempt to bring back the ark to Israel. Circle the things in 2 Samuel 6:1-5 that show how important this task must have been to the new king.

> *"David again assembled all the choice men in Israel, 30,000. He and all his troops set out to bring the ark of God from Baale-judah. The ark is called by the Name, the name of the LORD of Hosts who dwells between the cherubim. They set the ark of God on*

a new cart and transported it from Abinadab's house, which was on the hill. Uzzah
and Ahio, sons of Abinadab, were guiding the cart and brought it with the ark of
God from Abinadab's house on the hill. Ahio walked in front of the ark. David and
the whole house of Israel were celebrating before the LORD *with all kinds of fir wood*
instruments, lyres, harps, tambourines, sistrums, and cymbals" (2 Sam. 6:1-5).

The mantra of David's reign must be ours as well. "Bring back the ark of God to us!" is to be just as crucial and important to us as it was to David. This is a matter that cannot be taken lightly for the Christian who desires more than mere religion. Although no physical chest must sit in the center of our homes or cities to indicate God's presence, we must each make a personal decision to restore the centrality of God's presence and authority in the epicenter of our lives. We are the modern-day tabernacles in which God's presence dwells. We must centralize His authority in the practical rhythms of our lives. Just as David intended for the ark to sit squarely in the center of the nation, so must God be in the center of our daily living.

On the following chart record five decisions you have to make this week. They can be small ones or big ones. In the middle, record what would be your usual decision, and in the last column how that decision might be altered if you approach the decision with a God-awareness.

DECISION TO BE MADE	FIRST RESPONSE	GOD-AWARE RESPONSE
1		
2		
3		
4		
5		

A God-awareness or God-consciousness will indelibly imprint your life as it has mine. Just as being aware of a police officer nearby makes us cautious of our driving, awareness of God's presence will cause us to reconsider daily decisions we normally make. Reinstating God in the center of my existence has altered my choices in television shows, novels, movies, conversations, friendships, spending money, participation in offered opportunities, and so much more. It has often kept me from sidestepping tasks I would normally fear.

Once we begin to live aware of God with us in everything, we find that He really does have something to say about everything in our lives—not just the "Sunday morning" part but every other part as well. As we incorporate Him into our lives, He changes us on a very practical level.

"Lord, if Your presence does not go with us, do not lead us up from this place"
(Ex. 33:15).

Cassie knows this to be true. A stay-at-home mother of three little girls, she looks like an average soccer mom with few problems. Yet behind closed doors her life slowly fell apart. What began as occasional social drinks began to spiral out of control. She found herself drawn to the bottle in the morning, during the girls' nap times, and after she put them to bed in the evenings.

Finding a case of empty wine bottles she'd hidden from her husband startled her to the reality of her situation. She knew she needed help and sought wise counsel as well as the Lord's forgiveness and freedom from this addiction. Although she would have preferred an instant deliverance, it's been a daily process. It has not been easy, but she is dedicated to engaging in it by the Spirit's power and regaining control of her life. She has committed to starting every day by asking the Lord to remind her of His presence with her.

When Cassie feels the lure for the bottle, she takes a deep breath, remembers God's presence, and consciously seeks Him for assistance to make right choices. Her simple decisions to be aware of God throughout the regular rhythms of her day turned one day with no drinks into a week. That week became a month, and now she's well on her way to over a year of alcohol-free living.

Could a simple awareness of God's presence curb an alcohol addiction? Though I would never minimize the importance of assistance from credible outside sources when dealing with addiction, the answer in this case is a resounding yes! Many have testified that a God-consciousness can also save marriages, encourage better mothering, and spur righteous living in daily decision making.

A God-consciousness can make a serious practical impact on the decisions and circumstances in your life as well. Recognizing and acknowledging God's presence and perspective will alter your decisions and ultimately change outcomes.

FROM THE PAGES TO THE PRACTICAL

So how can we "bring back the ark of God"? Like David we must not just desire God's presence, but we also must make it our practical priority to restore the centrality of God's thinking and perspective into our everyday living. Depending on the season of life you are in, doing this will require your own unique path that you must map out for yourself.

9. Describe your current season of life. I would be an "at-home mom of young children."

As I write this lesson, I am on a 10-hour flight to Australia. While many would abhor being stuck on a plane for this long, I can barely contain my excitement. I haven't had such an extended period of quiet in years. I almost hate for the pilot to land this aircraft! What a joy it would be to spend one or two hours in the presence of God each day having uninterrupted quiet time. Let me tell you—in my life right now—that isn't happening.

Although my goal is to be alone with God every day, the demands of my season of life often interrupts my intentions. This inability to master my quiet time burdened me with an immense amount of guilt during my first years of mothering. I always felt "heavy" with condemnation that I wasn't spending enough time with God. It seemed to me that if I couldn't get an hour in then

10-15 minutes wasn't worth it. A godly woman helped me to remove that burden by directing me to an old book with a message for today. It is called *The Practice of the Presence of God* by Brother Lawrence. Intrigued by the title, I devoured it.

Although I was fascinated by the topic, I was also discouraged. The author wrote of his interludes with God while living at a monastery. Of course it would be easy for him to have a God-consciousness in a place like that, just like spending uninterrupted time with God is easy for me while I'm in a tube at 35,000 feet in the air. But then I discovered that this dear saint did indeed have a life like mine. His job at the monastery was kitchen duty. Cleaning the dishes, mopping floors, and disseminating meals were all his responsibilities throughout the day. His rendezvous with God weren't due to a schedule free from demands; they were in cooperation with them. So I was encouraged by a mentor and the book to incorporate my time with God throughout my day.

Here are a few things that some other mothers of small children and I have done to incorporate a God-consciousness into the regular rhythms of our day.

1. Print a Scripture verse or two in a large font and tape it on the bathroom mirror to meditate on while brushing little teeth and washing little hands. Use this same Scripture for seven days.
2. Pray breath prayers—sentence prayers as they come to you throughout the day.
3. Intentionally play worship music to contemplate while folding clothes or doing other tasks.
4. Wake up before the family and go for a walk or jog. Use this time not simply to exercise the body but also to talk to God and listen for His voice.
5. When outside with the children, ask them to point out a specific aspect of nature and what it might reveal about God's greatness to them. Pray with them in thanksgiving for God's creation.
6. Before getting out of bed each morning, offer yourself as a living sacrifice to God and ask Him specifically to make you aware of His presence throughout the day.
7. Every time you feel anxious or the need to worry, take that as a cue to offer the situation to God in prayer.

Think about your season of life and try to locate others in your group who have written down a similar season. Come up with a list of practical suggestions that you can incorporate into everyday living to assist you in being constantly aware of God's presence. Which one will you incorporate today?

Lord, today let me see You when You are moving and hear You when You are speaking. Heighten my spiritual sensitivities to notice Your activity around me, to me, and through me to others. May Your presence become so evident this day that I am steered clear of mistakes that I would most assuredly make if left to my own natural tendencies. Give me, dear Lord, a consciousness, an awareness of You everywhere and anywhere I may go.

WEEK ONE | DAY THREE

Sustained by God

"So David did exactly as God commanded him, and they struck down the Philistine army from Gibeon to Gezer" (1 Chron. 14:16, HCSB).

I've got a couple of problems I just can't seem to shake. Like Paul's thorn in the flesh, mine continually keep me at the feet of Jesus asking for His forgiveness and help. The first struggle has always been with my self-esteem. Masked by an outgoing and vivacious personality, I've spent most of my life never feeling good enough at just being myself.

Every season of life has brought demands that I am sure God gave me by mistake since He must know I could never handle the task. In everything from being a mom to teaching God's Word I've regretted that God didn't know better than to ask me to undertake the responsibility.

When I'm not struggling with my sense of worth, I'm working hard to "let go and let God." A sweet older woman from my church hugged me this past Sunday, and said, "I'm so glad you turned into something good. You were such a bossy little thing!" Honey, I haven't grown out of it! Though I might not tell people what to do right out, my husband says I have a sneaky way of asking the same questions until I manipulate the answer I want. I usually don't even recognize my tendency to control until I'm so tired from juggling all the balls that I fumble one.

Do you have issues with either esteem or control? If you are like most humans, then you probably do to some degree. Get ready to dive in deep to take a look at how David's story gives us some assistance to begin to relinquish both to God. Yesterday we looked at 1 Chronicles 14:2 and the decisions David made as the new king because of it. Two precious principles from this verse offer us keen insight into our own battle with identity and the need to control. Today we focus on control issues and tomorrow on our worth in light of God's Word.

1. Write 1 Chronicles 14:2 in your own words and recall the main principles from the three questions about the verse at the beginning of yesterday's lesson.

David's confidence was in God as his true source. If anyone had a reason to struggle with control issues and have a warped sense of self, it was David at this point in his life. I am amazed that a man in the highest position of royalty and authority in the nation would have such regard for God. Humans tend to become more self-sufficient the more we achieve success, yet David illustrates the opposite. He was certain that Yahweh was the source of his life and that his ability to perform well resulted from God's grace.

THE SOURCE AND SUSTAINER

One of my favorite gospel songs is "Total Praise" by Richard Smallwood. Every time my church choir starts swaying to the soulful beat and belting out those piercing harmonies, I'm reminded of the source of my strength and life and what my response should be. For believers who truly see the Lord calling the shots and regulating their existence, the response should be to throw up their hands in surrender (We take that literally at my church!) and trust God to bring about His best outcome in life's circumstances.

2. What do you seek for control in your life?

❑ Other people

❑ Your friends' actions

❑ Others' responses

❑ Your daily schedule

❑ Outcome of circumstances or events

❑ Your husband's responses and decisions

❑ Your adult children's behavior

❑ God's response or timing

❑ Family dynamics

❑ Other

3. In the face of great adversity, what actions in 1 Chronicles 14:9-16 reveal David's desire to trust God for ultimate control?

We say God is in control. We sing songs about trusting Him, but what a difference in the person who lives like God is the source and sustainer. In spite of full lives, somehow they still seem at rest. They aren't exhausted from a life filled with anxiety as they seek to control people and events. They are also not frustrated when things don't go as they had hoped. They are satisfied with the rewards of obeying God and rest easy in knowing that the outcome was given and allowed by a God who loves them and has their best interest in mind.

4. List two people you know who seem to do a good job trusting God to control things.

What attributes characterize their existence?

George Muller said, "The beginning of anxiety is the end of faith. The beginning of true faith is the end of anxiety."[3] Our anxiety always stems from a desire to control and indicates that we have ceased to trust the Lord. When we are depending on the Lord to handle the people and circumstances in our lives, the outcome will be an existence virtually free from worry, anxiety, and fear. Peace will begin to flow like a river in our everyday living. Jesus put it this way:

> *"And if God cares so wonderfully for wildflowers that are here today and thrown into the fire tomorrow, he will certainly care for you. Why do you have so little faith? So don't worry about these things, saying, 'What will we eat? What will we drink? What will we wear?' These things dominate the thoughts of unbelievers, but your heavenly Father already knows all your needs"* (Matt. 6:30-32, NLT).

5. Rate your level of anxiety in each of the following areas with 1 being the least amount of worry and 5 being off the chart levels of worry.

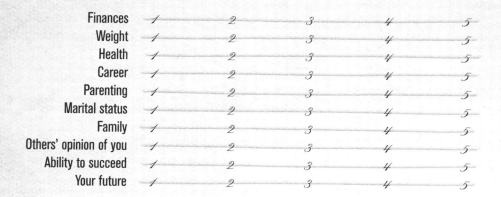

	1	2	3	4	5
Finances					
Weight					
Health					
Career					
Parenting					
Marital status					
Family					
Others' opinion of you					
Ability to succeed					
Your future					

6. What does your level of worry reveal to you about your faith in God in each area?

TAKE A LOAD OFF

Sometimes I feel as if the weight of the world is on my shoulders, don't you? And it can be overwhelming, can't it? Imagine the emotional weight on David had he believed the whole nation rested on his shoulders. Rather, David knew it was his responsibility to seek God—as we will see him demonstrate later in the story in 1 Chronicles 14—listen for His instructions, and respond in obedience. After that, the outcome was ultimately God's responsibility. As a result, David wasn't anxious or consumed by fear even when surrounded by fierce enemies seeking to destroy him.

Second Samuel 1 clearly demonstrates how David's release of control to God affected his life in practical ways. This story takes place before he became king of Judah, the southern portion of Israel. Under the circumstances it would seem that news of the Philistines defeating Israel and slaying its current leader, Saul, would have brought joy to David. Now it would finally be his turn to reign. Yet instead of moving forward to claim the throne, David did two things:

7. Look up the following passages and record the two things David did:

   2 Samuel 1:12,17

   2 Samuel 2:1

8. According to the time line from yesterday's lesson, how much time lapsed between when David was anointed king and when he began his initial reign at Judah?

How different David's response was from what mine might have been in this type of situation! After waiting so many years to see God make good on His promise to me, I most likely would have impatiently grumbled while waiting for the first opening to force my way into what I thought should be my rightful position. When circumstances arose that seemed to finally give me an opportunity, I can't imagine that I would weep for others and then seek God before moving. I might be more inclined to secretly applaud their demise while planning my triumphal entry into their former positions.

9. **Compare David's actions in this story with Rebekah and Jacob's in Genesis 27:1-25. What types of deceitful actions did this duo engage in to control the situation and manipulate it to their advantage?**

10. **How does this differ from David in 2 Samuel 3?**

11. **Peace characterizes the person who trusts God. What do you think will characterize a person who seeks to control and manipulate circumstances?**

Controlling people, circumstances, and outcomes has become too exhausting for me. I experience intense anxiety when I try to be in charge of more than I'm meant to handle. Trusting God lifts our load, and sweet peace and rest become available to all who will relinquish control and allow Him to do what He does best—be Himself—the Source and Sustainer of our lives.

> *"Be anxious for nothing, but in everything by prayer and supplication with thanksgiving let your requests be made known to God. And the peace of God, which surpasses all comprehension, will guard your hearts and your minds in Christ Jesus"*
> (Phil. 4:6-7, NASB).

End this lesson by recording one thing that you would normally seek to control today. Ask the Lord to lift the load of this burden from your shoulders as you release the ultimate outcome of that situation or person to Him. What can you choose to do or not do today that will show you trust in God in that situation?

WEEK ONE | DAY FOUR
Established By God

*"It is not that we are qualified to do anything on our own.
Our qualification comes from God" (2 Cor. 3:5, NLT).*

Sharing the platform with Beth Moore and Kay Arthur has been one of the highlights of my life. It is a privilege to sit under their teaching. Listening to them has heightened my respect for the proclamation of God's Word and deepened my walk with Him. I'd much rather keep my seat and listen to those two than take my turn behind the microphone, not merely because I enjoy their ministries but because I feel a level of intimidation sharing a platform with great women of God like these. How would you feel teaching a Bible study where one of them is seated on the front row? You've got it, Sister! That's exactly how I feel: humbled and scared to death. Thankfully, they are both patient mentors and friends who are unendingly gracious and kind.

How can I—how can we—walk confidently into situations we feel ill-equipped to handle? How will we stand on the platforms to which God has called us and face the crowd in our lives without shame over who we are and without fear about our ability to accomplish the task? We must come to our situations knowing that God equips for His purpose those He calls. He didn't select us to lead the study, mother the children, marry the man, lead the meeting, run the office, evangelize the tribe, or start the ministry because He knew we were already capable. Rather, He picked us up, dusted off our incapability, replaced it with His ability, and secured our success when we chose to rest and trust in Him to work supernaturally in us.

*"Not that we are adequate in ourselves to consider anything as coming
from ourselves, but our adequacy is from God, who also made us adequate
as servants of a new covenant" (2 Cor. 3:5-6, NASB).*

1. See if you can finish from memory these statements from the first three lessons.

    Day 1: David was _____ by God. Likewise, I have been _____ by God.

    Day 2: As a chosen vessel, the mantra of David's life was _____. Likewise, the mantra of my life must be _____. I do this by living each day with a God-_____.

    Day 3: David recognized God as the _____ and _____ of His life and therefore the weight of the kingdom did not rest on His shoulders. Likewise, God is the _____ and _____ of my life.

You have been handpicked by God to be in relationship and in service to Him (1 Chron. 14:2). Your success depends on the centrality of God's authority in your life. As you live with a God-consciousness, remembering that He is the Source and Sustainer of your existence, He will relieve you of the need to control others and circumstances. Without the weight of the world on your shoulders, you can enjoy what God's children were meant to enjoy.

2. What is one thing in your life right now that you feel most ill-equipped to handle? Why?

THE ESTABLISHER

Yesterday we saw God as the Source and Sustainer of David's life. Today we see the outcome of this relationship. Chronicles tells us that the Lord established him. Along with its derivatives, the root of this word is used 288 times in the Bible. The root meaning is to bring something into being with the consequence that its existence is a certainty.[4]

When God is the subject of the verb establish (as in 1 Chron. 14:2), it means that He sets things securely in order and prepares them for the specified purpose.

Look at that meaning again and let the truth of what this meant for David sink deeply into your consciousness.

> *"Do you thus repay the LORD, O foolish and unwise people? Is not He your Father who has bought you? He has made you and established you"* (Deut. 32:6, NASB).

3. Using our definition for *established*, write a statement about what God did for David by establishing him in 1 Chronicles 14:2.

What the Lord calls, He establishes. That is: He brings into existence and assures the ability for the outcome to fulfill His purposes and plans. When God establishes a person for a specific purpose, as He did in David's case, He secures, equips, and fortifies the person called so that he or she is fully capable of performing the task at hand. My personal tendency to feel ill-equipped and insufficient is in direct correlation to my lack of belief that I have been established and equipped by God to accomplish the task.

My esteem and yours is wrapped up in our faith that we are established by an Almighty God to accomplish His purposes. If we are trusting in our own capabilities to handle the tasks at hand, then we should be intimidated and fearful; but if we are resting in God's work in us, then this outlook will produce different results. Believing God has called and established you is fundamental to living with a valid sense of worth and fulfilling God's purposes in your life.

4. Do you believe you have been established by God to handle the purposes He has given to you? Yes ❏ No ❏
   Why or why not?

Bobbie Houston knows this all too well. She says that her journey began as a simple whisper from the mouth of God to her listening soul. She sensed the Lord leading her to give women the message that He exists and that He loves and believes in them. She didn't know the details of what He was asking or how she would pull it off. But she felt led to start a sisterhood of women from different cultures and nations who were sold out for the cause of Christ and the difference He can make in the practical everyday lives of others.

Twelve years later the whisper has grown into a resounding roar that can be heard from the corners of Sydney, Australia, to the blue skies of London as nearly 20,000 women gather each year to celebrate God and to strengthen their resolve to make a strategic difference in the lives of others in need throughout the coming year. Bobbie will tell you that her normally timid, sedate, and retiring personality would never have allowed her to step into this position of leadership. But accompanying God's call was a unique empowering to accomplish the task that He had purposed for her to do before the foundation of the world. Her only job was to trust in His Spirit and act in obedience to what He had called her to. Her obedience has reaped stunning rewards.

> *"But the Lord is faithful, and He will strengthen and protect you from the evil one"*
> *(2 Thess. 3:3, NASB).*

5. **Consider the following illustrations and answer the corresponding questions:**

   What did God ask Moses to do (Ex. 3:4-16)?

   Why did he feel unable to do it and how did God equip him?

   What did God ask Jeremiah to do (Jer. 1:4-10)?

   Why didn't he want to do it, and how did God enable him?

   What did God ask King Solomon to do? (1 Kings 3:6-12)

   Why did he feel ill-equipped to do it, and how did God enable him?

6. **To which of these three illustrations do you most relate? Why?**

   > *"[He] has granted to us everything pertaining to life and godliness" (2 Pet. 1:3, NASB).*

God seems to specialize in putting us in positions where we must rely on His work in us. I often recognize God's leading specifically because He calls me to do something I am afraid to do. I'm learning that when God wants to show Himself in living color, He works through us. He purposefully puts us in a place where we will have to depend on Him to accomplish the task at hand, therefore seeing His greatness and turning our worship more fully toward Himself.

CREATED ANEW
7. **Read Ephesians 2:10 below. Circle the word that describes the believer.**

*"For we are God's masterpiece. He has created us anew in Christ Jesus so we
can do good things he planned for us long ago" (Eph. 2:10, NLT).*

What word does your translation of the Bible use in place of this one?

What immediate mental pictures do these words bring to your mind?

The word *workmanship* or *masterpiece* in this verse is used figuratively to illustrate a literal
principle. Romans 1:20 reveals the literal usage of this word.

8. What phrase Romans 1:20 do you think matches in workmanship Ephesians 2:10?

Paul said God's great attributes and glorious characteristics are revealed in "what has been made"
or His workmanship as displayed in nature. He established the earth (Ps. 119:90) and set it
securely in place so that through it His glory could be seen. He establishes and equips believers
for the same purpose. When you receive Christ, He re-creates you in Christ Jesus. Only His
predesigned good works will bring Him glory, and our participation in these good works are
impossible apart from His new creation.

9. What is the main purpose of God's workmanship?

**10. At the beginning of this lesson you wrote down the one thing in your life you feel ill-
equipped to handle. Now fill in these blanks to restate your position and to begin to
renew your thinking in this area of your life.**

**I feel completely ill-equipped to accomplish _____. But in accordance
with God's Word I, _____(your name), fully believe that I have been created
_____ and equipped by God to fulfill that purpose. I am not capable in my flesh but
according to 2 Corinthians 3:5-6, by God's _____ I have been made _____.
As His workmanship, my main purpose is to _____.**

*"Let your light so shine before men, that they may see your good works, and
glorify your Father which is in heaven" (Matt. 5:16, NASB).*

Recognizing God as your establisher is the cure for any self-esteem issue. For those like myself
who struggle with thinking too lowly of themselves, knowing that you are equipped by God gives
you a God-confidence. For the one who struggles with thinking too highly of themselves than
they ought, this principle is a constant reminder that apart from God's choosing and equipping,
the success you've achieved in any area of your life would have been an impossibility.

"But by the grace of God I am what I am" (1 Cor. 15:10).

WEEK ONE | DAY FIVE

Positioned for a Purpose

*"For David, **after serving his own generation in God's plan, fell asleep, and was buried with his fathers**" (Acts 13:36, HCSB).*

Our two sons, Jerry, and I were all sick for two-and-one-half months straight. The injustice of flu season invaded our home with a mighty vengeance. One of our boys brought the bug home from mother's day out, and we just passed it back and forth. I will never forget the long nights and days as Jerry and I tried to take care of our sick toddlers while fighting symptoms of our own. It was awful. As soon as one started to feel better, another would begin to feel worse.

We visited our family doctor no less than six times during those months. Each time one of us would have the actual appointment, but we'd all tag along so our gracious doctor could check all four throats, four noses, and eight ears. The fifth visit was primarily for me. I sat on the thin white paper that garnished the patient bed in the office and waited for him. My head was throbbing from exhaustion and sickness. When Dr. Bruce walked in, he was his normal cheery self. He gave me a sympathetic look, asked me how I was feeling, and began his exam.

I suddenly realized his unbelievable health during this invasive season of the flu. Every time we'd been in his office he was perfectly well. How did he see sick people like us day after day, work in such close contact with so many germs, and maintain his health at the same time? I had to know and so I asked. Dr. Bruce sat back in his swivel chair thoughtfully then said, "I could tell you about vitamins that I take or something like that, but honestly, Priscilla, my wife and I really believe that God keeps us healthy so that we can help those who are not. It's the only explanation we can figure."

God keeps us healthy … to help those who are not.

Dr. Bruce knows what Scripture teaches again and again: Our God is one of purpose and intent, and He intends to impact the lives of people. He never gives a blessing, extends a gift, offers an opportunity, or creates a solution without a specific purpose. Those whom God has handpicked for a specific calling, established with His power, and anointed by His Spirit have been given that privilege of being a conduit through which those blessings can flow to others.

David recognized that His specific anointing to the unique position as king was not a decision made by God without deliberate intentions. He knew specific people in his generation were to be beneficiaries of his divine calling.

1. According to 1 Chronicles 14:2, for whose sake was David made king?

This week we've considered your standing as a handpicked, established, and anointed believer God has called for specific tasks in this generation. I want to end this week by turning your attention to the foundational purpose for which you were called. The assignment itself is never the bottom line of God's choosing you. His goal is that through your full obedience to His call specific people in your generations will be blessed and encouraged to follow Him more fully.

2. On page 27 you listed a task you believe God has divinely equipped you to handle. Write that task along with another one that you know He has made you capable of doing.

3. What questions do you find yourself asking God about why He has allowed these circumstances in this season of your life?

The Father loves people, not programs. Any program He initiates and or assignment He commissions you to do always has this as its main goal turning people to a relationship with Himself. Mothering is not the ultimate goal of being a mom, revealing Christ to the children is. The position of leader in the career or ministry is not the goal, those in your sphere of influence seeing God's love reflected in you is. Regardless of the scenario, God wants to reveal Himself to individuals and uses other individuals as a conduit for this to happen.

From the beginning of time God has made this passion clear. In the Old Testament He loved the Hebrews with a jealous love (Ex. 34:14), and in the New Testament He even sent His own Son to walk among us in the flesh so that we could be drawn more fully to Him. Now, when He works through us, anointing us for divine purposes, His intention is not the task but that He might be more clearly seen. Remembering this goal of affecting people's lives will help us be diligent when the task to which we have been called becomes challenging.

CALLED TO A NATION

One of the clearest illustrations of God's calling someone to a specific assignment to have a specific impact on a group of people is found in Exodus 3. Moses was 80 years old, alone in a barren wilderness, and watching over a flock of sheep when God met Him in a unique way.

> *"The angel of the LORD appeared to him in a blazing fire from the midst of a bush; and he looked, and behold, the bush was burning with fire, yet the bush was not consumed" (Ex. 3:2, NASB).*

As he recognized God's presence, Moses immediately removed his sandals in reverence. With his attention turned toward the Holy One, the Lord called Moses into His service—from shepherd of sheep to shepherd of people.

Moses' response reminds me of mine when God gives me an assignment I feel ill-equipped to handle. He recounted his inability to accomplish the task and reminded God that others might be more suited for the endeavor. Yet God persisted because freedom, deliverance, and intimacy with Yahweh would come to these people through Moses.

In this generation certain people have been assigned and entrusted to you, dear believer. Your unbridled obedience to God is paramount to their seeing the divine hand of God in their lives. So get busy with the program while keeping your eyes squarely on the people.

4. **Choose two of the following examples and explore what God called that person to do and who was to benefit from their obedience in pursuing that calling.**

   Paul: Acts 9:3-6,13-16; Ephesians 3:1,6-8

   What were the circumstances around Paul's calling?

   For what purpose was he called?

   How would his obedience affect the people he was called to serve?

   Esther: Esther 2:4-9; 3:13; 4:13-16; 8:11-17

   What were the circumstances around Esther's calling?

   For what purpose was she called?

   What would the consequences be to others had she not submitted to God's calling?

   Abraham: Genesis 12:1-3

   What were the circumstances around Abraham's calling?

   For what purpose was he called?

   What people were to be affected by him walking in that purpose?

Jesus: Luke 4:18

What were the circumstances around Jesus' calling?

For what purpose was He called?

What people were to be affected by Him walking in that purpose?

In each of these cases the calling itself was not the main purpose and thrust of the mission for which they were sent. The task was not to be an end in itself.

• In calling Paul, God wanted the Gentiles to be saved.
• In commissioning Esther, the Jews would be rescued.
• In choosing Abraham, a nation was to be created through which the Savior would be born.
• And in sending Jesus, the Father allowed the worst possible torture—death on a cross—to draw all men to Himself.

Do you see, even in the case of His own Son, the mission of dying on the cross would have been fruitless if the end result didn't produce a means through which you and I could be saved? We were His purpose. In every circumstance the purpose was not a program. The purpose was people.

PURPOSED FOR PEOPLE

I've noticed that I often tend to lean toward the programming over the people involved. I can tell this because when I'm cooking dinner for my family or folding their laundry, I can easily become irritated when my children or husband interrupt me and need my attention. When I was engrossed in planning a bridal shower for a close friend, I remember feeling frustrated when she called me to meet for lunch during a very busy week. In each case I allowed my attention on the task to override the relationship for which I was doing it.

5. Are you normally more geared toward:
   * Relationships with people? or   * Tasks and programs?

6. How is this evident in your life? If you are not certain, ask a close friend to give you an honest assessment.

7. How do you think you can find a healthy balance between the two?

8. You previously listed two tasks God has called you to undertake in this season of your life. For each one determine how you might use these divine tasks to bless others and the persons whose lives will most likely be affected if you are follow through on those assignments.

Divine Assignment	Plan to Bless	People Affected
task #1		
task #2		

Whether the people you listed above are loved ones or a group of folks with whom you are not very familiar, each has been strategically placed in your life so that your obedience to God's call can cause them to see Christ more fully and personally. This is your goal.

"Let your light shine before men in such a way that they may see your good works, and glorify your Father who is in heaven" (Matt. 5:16, NASB).

MY STORY

My family and I have lived in the same neighborhood for nine years, and we've had the same wonderful neighbors the entire time. To our left, Oscar and Maryann have been the best next-door neighbors we could ever ask for. For years we'd see both of them every day as they worked in the yard and went on walks. They were there to offer milk, eggs, and sugar when I was running low and even watch our home and pick up our mail when we were traveling. Maryann took a special interest in my boys. As a retired teacher she loved to ring my doorbell and grab the children when there was something interesting happening in nature. If there were a caterpillar hatching from a cocoon or an interesting plant sprouting from the ground, she wanted them to see it and learn a thing or two.

For years I sensed God asking me to question them about their salvation. On many occasions I felt that internal burning that accompanies God's voice telling me to invite them to church and share the gospel without hesitation. Thinking that there would always be more time later, I delayed.

It was warm day two years ago that my husband came home and walked into our bedroom with a blank look on his face. He let out a huge sigh and told me that he'd just been talking to Oscar in the front yard. Oscar had been stunned to wake up that morning to find that Maryann had died during the night. I was completely shocked. I had just seen her the day before and talked with her over the flowers she was planting. How could she be gone so abruptly? I walked over to Oscar's house. Tears rolled down his elderly face as I hugged his neck and shared his grief.

I mourned the loss of my friend in the days to come, and my heart was torn with conviction as the Holy Spirit reminded me of His repeated attempts to get me to talk with her about the Lord. She had been entrusted to me as a neighbor and a friend. My purpose for living in that neighborhood for nine years was not just about my own family; it was about hers. I wept over her loss and over my lack of spiritual awareness to recognize the purpose for which God may have wanted me there.

9. **From the names you listed as your divine assignment, choose one individual on whom you can specifically focus your efforts this week. Ask the Lord to show you how to be a blessing to that person. As the Lord speaks to you in the days to come, fill in the blanks below.**

   Name of individual _____

   What I plan to do to be a blessing to him or her _____

   Date I performed this task _____

   His or her response _____

   My response_____

1. Kenneth S. Wuest. *Wuest's Word Studies from the Greek New Testament: For the English Reader* (Grand Rapids, MI: Eerdmans, 1997, c1984), 34.

2. Class notes on 1,2 Samuel by Dr. Steven Bramer, Dallas Theological Seminary.

3. Linda Dillow. *Calm My Anxious Heart: A Woman's Guide to Finding Contentment* (Colorado Springs, CO: Navpress Publishing Group, 1998), 123.

4. R. Laird Harris; Robert Laird Harris; Gleason Leonard Archer; Bruce K. Waltke. *Theological Wordbook of the Old Testament.* electronic ed. (Chicago: Moody Press, 1999), 433.

VIEWERGUIDE

THE ANOINTING: DIRECTED AND GUARANTEED

1. God is not looking for _____ women. He is looking for _____ women.

2. We have a Father whose heart for us is _____.

3. Having a God awareness is going to _____ you something and cause you to make decisions that you would not normally make.

4. The enemy has a three-part game plan to_____, _____, and _____ (John 10:10).

5. The anointing not only guarantees you opposition, but it also guarantees you _____ _____ _____.

6. David's example shows us that the most important thing that we can have is a fresh, ongoing, intimate _____ with God.

7. The anointing not only guarantees you opposition and access to God but it also guarantees you specific, divine _____ from God.

8. The more you know God, the more clearly you will be able to _____ Him.

9. The anointed are not only guaranteed opposition, access to God, and specific, divine direction from God, but also we are guaranteed supernatural _____ when we obey God.

GROUP DISCUSSION QUESTIONS

1. We as believers have access to God. How do we have access to God? What can we expect as a result of that access?

2. What are some of your favorite promises from God's Word?

ANOINTED

WEEK TWO | DAY ONE

The Anointing

"Then Samuel took the horn of oil and anointed him in the midst of his brothers; and the Spirit of the LORD came mightily upon David from that day forward" (1 Sam. 16:13).

For three days in May 2007 I slept on the couch in my grandparents' living room along with my sister, aunt, and mother. Inches from the hospice bed, we all watched my 90-year-old grandfather dying before our eyes. I spent time sitting at his side, rubbing his hands, talking to him, and listening to his last words. For months we'd known his kidneys were failing and his time with us would be coming to an end soon. It appeared that this weekend would be his last. His kidneys had stopped processing the fluids in his body, so now it was filling with water. As his lungs became completely covered in fluid, he would violently awaken, drowning in his own fluids. When he could finally catch his breath from coughing, he would speak a few feeble words. In an effort to capture his thoughts, I recorded everything he said.

"Praise the Lord."
"Thank God for His love."
"God is good."
"I see the Lord. Yes. I see Him."

"It's a wonderful thing to know the Lord."
"I just can't stop praising Him."
"Wonderful Savior."

Tears rolled down our cheeks as we thought of life without Grandpa, but mostly we celebrated the godly life of this family patriarch who led us all into deeper relationships with the Lord. And now, standing at the very doorway of death, his every word and every thought was still focused and fully led by the Spirit of the living God. Full of life in the face of death: He was the picture of an anointed believer filled to overflowing with the Holy Spirit.

How can we face life's most crushing challenges with God's praise on our lips and His confidence in our choices? Being directed, comforted, and empowered by His Spirit within us is the only sure way to live with supernatural success when we encounter natural events that seek to derail us. We must be anointed.

THE ANOINTING: WHAT IS IT?

The term *anointing* has taken a lot of flack. Tossed around so loosely, it seems to have lost its intended meaning and credibility. We aren't sure if only a unique few experience anointing or if we all have access to its fruits. We don't know what we have to do to get it or if we even want it, since we often hear it mentioned along with ridiculously weird occurrences. Veiled by a cloud of suspicion, we've pushed it aside and silenced its importance and necessity in our Christian lives.

David's rule brings anointing back to the forefront of our minds as we look at 1 Chronicles 14. In fact, we can't escape it, for it's tucked in verses 8 to the end of the chapter. We see the windfall of consequences anointing brings in David's story—in our story.

The anointing on David's life was essential to accomplish God's purposes, and we must have it to accomplish His plans for us. Without it, everything we do will only be a shell of activity that will leave us breathless from a series of frustrated efforts, amounting to little. With God's anointing we can face life's circumstances with courage, joy, and inner peace. Last week we dug into 1 Chronicles 14:2. Now let's see how the rest of the story unfolds beginning in verse 8.

> *"When the Philistines heard that David had been anointed king over all Israel"*
> *(1 Chron. 14:8, NASB).*

God established David by a symbolic display. The prophet Samuel delivered God's anointing.

1. Read 1 Samuel 16:1-13 and answer the following questions:

  * Who sent the prophet Samuel to anoint David (v. 1)?
  * Who did Samuel think God's choice was (v. 6)?
  * Why did he think this (v. 7)?
  * Who did Jesse think God's choice was (vv. 8-10)?
  * Why didn't Jesse think David was an option for the anointing (v. 11)?
  * Who was present to see David receive the anointing (v. 13)?
  * What might be the importance of this?

To David's family, Samuel's pouring the oil symbolized unique calling and divine appointment. The verb *to anoint* and its derivatives appear over 140 times throughout the Scriptures. The word *anointed* comes from the Hebrew word *mashach*. The word is used for the ceremonial induction into leadership offices by the pouring of oil from a horn on the head of an individual.

Anointing set apart and consecrated a person to divine service. Anointing with oil was often accompanied by another important and interesting spiritual event. When Samuel anointed David, the Spirit of God rested on him in a new way from that day forward to empower and strengthen him for the particular task at hand (see 1 Sam. 16:13). Anointing means "a divine enablement to accomplish a divine task or a supernatural empowering to accomplish supernatural goals."

GOD'S ANOINTING IN US

God's goals and plans for us require His power. In our natural abilities we might be able to teach the class, mother the children, stay in the marriage, or write the book, but to fulfill the supernatural purposes of these natural activities demands an anointing by God's Spirit.

* The anointing causes a woman with children to become a developer of Christian soldiers.
* The anointing gives a mere speaker a message that penetrates the hearts of the listeners.
* An author can pen a book without the anointing, but only the anointed author can write words that carry the weight of God to accomplish eternal purposes in the lives of readers.

David, the mere shepherd boy given a throne, was established by God and anointed for His service. David accomplished supernatural kingdom purposes because God's Spirit equipped him for the tasks. Enabled by God, he led the people like no other. As believers, God calls us to accomplish divine tasks for His glory. We must have the anointing of God's Spirit.

2. Paul showed the connection between David's life and ours in 2 Corinthians 1:21-22. Copy these verses from your Bible.

According to these verses, those who place faith in Christ are not only established but also anointed by God. As David was endowed with the Spirit's presence from the day of his anointing, we have been anointed with the indwelling Spirit's presence from the day of our salvation. Ephesians 1:13-14 makes it clear to us that this anointing by the Holy Spirit occurs the moment we believe in Christ for salvation from our sins.

> *"In Him, you also, after listening to the message of truth, the gospel of your salvation—having also believed, you were sealed in Him with the Holy Spirit of promise, who is given as a pledge of our inheritance" (Eph. 1:13-14, NASB).*

The Spirit lives in us, and we are sealed and anointed by Him to accomplish God's preplanned purposes. So, if you are a believer, you are anointed—right now. Your task is to rely on the power of God who indwells you so you can be empowered to do what you cannot do on your own. The Spirit's presence in our lives brings many benefits, but three main purposes relate to our study. We are anointed by the Spirit to:

- Authenticate divine ownership: We belong to God and God belongs to us.
- Guarantee divine completion: We are kept by God until the day of His return.
- Empower for divine purpose: We are equipped to accomplish supernatural tasks.

3. Look up the following verses and match each to its corresponding Spirit's purpose.

1. Romans 5:5 and 2 Corinthians 5:5	____ Divine Empowerment
2. Romans 8:9 and 1 Corinthians 6:19-20	____ Divine Completion
3. Luke 1:35 and Acts 1:8	____ Divine Ownership

In Old Testament times a seal from the author authenticated a letter. The Holy Spirit seals or authenticates your relationship to God. We have been sealed by God and belong to Him. The Spirit's presence is the anointing, guaranteeing that He who has begun a good work will be faithful to complete it until the day of Christ Jesus (Phil. 1:6).

ANOINTED FOR MIRACULOUS LIVING

By no means am I suggesting that the Spirit-filled life sees miraculous events at the snap of a finger. Those waiting on a life of continuous miracles as a sign of God's anointing will lead a frustrated existence as they try to manipulate God. On the contrary, the anointed life engages daily and normal activities in a supernatural way. When you have patience in your mothering, holiness in your singleness, gentleness in your response, contentment in your circumstances, and empowerment in the face of your challenges, you are experiencing the greatest miracle of all: God's presence appearing in your life.

In *Flying Closer to the Flame,* Chuck Swindoll lists marks of a Spirit-filled life.[1] I've given some of them below. Although we never reach perfection in these areas, they are great guidelines.

We have an inner dynamic to handle life's pressures.
We can be joyful … regardless.
We have the capacity to grasp the deep things of God that He discloses to us in His Book.
We have little difficulty maintaining a positive attitude of unselfishness, servanthoood, and humility.
We have a keen sense of intuition and discernment; we sense evil.
We can love and be loved in return.
We don't need to fear evil or demonic and satanic assault.
We are enabled to stand alone in confidence.
We experience inner assurance regarding decisions as well as right and wrong.
We can actually live worry-free.
We are able to minister to others through our spiritual gift(s).
We have an intimate, abiding "Abba relationship" with the living God.

4. **Look carefully at Swindoll's list and consider your life in relationship to these things. Put a plus sign beside the ones most evidenced in your life and a minus sign beside those least evidenced.**

5. **In the following chart write down tasks that you undertake in your life, the part you can do in your natural ability, and then the part you can only accomplish through the anointing of God's Spirit. I've given you an illustration from my own life.**

The Task	The Natural Accomplishment	The Anointed Accomplishment
Mother two small children	*Take care of their daily needs and provide a home for them*	*Instill in them a love for the Lord and a desire serve Him*

Friend, if you know Jesus, you are anointed—empowered to live supernaturally for the purpose of accomplishing God's tasks on the earth. Believers led and enabled by God's Spirit can accomplish His plans and purposes. Our attempts may achieve stunning success in the natural realm but will not amount to much in God's economy.

6. **As you close today's lesson, consider the task you wrote on page 25 as something you know God has called you to in this season of life but feel ill-equipped to handle. Thank Him for anointing you at the moment of your salvation for this task and ask Him to help you to tap into the power of His Spirit.**

WEEK TWO | DAY TWO
Opposition to the Anointing

"A thief comes only to steal and to kill and to destroy. I have come that they may have life and have it in abundance" (John 10:10).

On my regular walk I decided to take a new route through some neighboring trails near a duck pond. I wove in and out of the woods, over bridges, and under man-made wooden overpasses. I took my eyes off of the road for a split second to close them, turn my chin upward, and enjoy the warmth of the sun on my face. A violent rustling in the brush just two feet away jolted my attention back to ground level. I jumped away from the noise just in time to escape the dog that lunged out from the bush line. I stopped in my tracks and fear gripped my heart. He barked voraciously while showing all of his teeth in a mouth dripping with froth.

The local morning news that had headlined with a story of a young boy being viciously attacked and killed by a crazed dog flashed into my mind. I knew for sure I would be next. My heart raced and sweat began to bead above my brow. I knew if I ran, he would be incited to run after me, so I grabbed a stick from the ground and stood as still as I could with my palms out in front of me. He never stopped barking and never seemed to back down. I wondered if a neighbor would hear the commotion and come to help me. No one ever did. I was on my own.

As the seconds rolled on the dog didn't tire, yet I noticed that he never lunged at me. Not once did he try to take a bite. I realized that this barking maniac was a menacing figure indeed, but he didn't seem to put his money where his mouth was. I thought that the only way to see if I was correct would be to lunge toward him with a stick and see if he would cower in fear. I girded my courage, took a deep breath, and screamed at the top of my lungs while taking a huge leap in his direction. My behavior was more than this panicked dog had planned for. He recoiled, darted into the bushes, and ran away. All that bravado without any of the bite.

We have an enemy. He seeks to divert us from the course set for us by our Father. Once we are saved, our enemy cannot destroy us, but he will work hard to distract us. It seems he most likes to startle us when we have just closed our eyes and turned our chins upward to enjoy a sunny patch in our existence. Without warning, he jumps from around a corner and terrifies us with his rabid barking. We tremble in our spiritual boots, certain he will be our demise.

We do well to remember that this enemy is all bravado and no bite. No matter how good he is at barking, he has already been rendered impotent. One full-on authoritative, victorious leap by the powerful people of God will send him running, shaking in his boots all the way.

OPPOSITION TO THE ANOINTING

At salvation all believers are anointed, and yet many do not live in accordance with this great power they have been given. Instead of tapping into God's divine empowering to live the abundant life promised in Scripture, they seek to live in their own power and strength detached from the lifeline of God within. This leaves them depleted, frustrated, and less capable of handling the Enemy's attacks.

And make no mistake about it … the Enemy will attack. In fact, his attacks are more sure to happen to those who determine to fully engage in living the anointed life.

> "Stay alert! Watch out for your great enemy, the devil. He prowls around like
> a roaring lion, looking for someone to devour" (1 Pet. 5:8, NLT).

1. Complete the following Scripture from 1 Chronicles 14:8.

   "When the _____ heard that David had been _____ king over all of Israel, _____ of the Philistines went up _____."

2. From your time line on page 14, how long was David king of the Southern Kingdom of Judah before he became king over the entire nation of Israel?

No record tells of the Philistines attacking David until he began to walk in the full appointment of his calling. Even when he reigned in southern Israel, they didn't bother him. But when he became king over all of Israel and accessing the fullness of God's anointing, his enemies got stirred up and took action.

3. In what areas of your life do you sense the most spiritual resistance?

4. How can you see the hand of your enemy behind this opposition?

5. How can you see opposition as a sign of God's working through you?

PREPARED FOR COMBAT

In John 10:10 Jesus said He came to offer abundant life. In the same verse He explained that the believer should be on guard. He said that the Enemy is out to steal, kill, and destroy. Christians must be prepared for the Enemy and the game plan he has used since the beginning of time.

6. What similar word indicating the action required by the believer facing spiritual opposition appears in James 4:7; 1 Peter 5:9; and Ephesians 6:13?

These verses use warfare terminology. They give an active command to soldiers of the Lord, telling us to turn from our current position and engage the Enemy in the battle. Scripture doesn't command a futile and feeble attempt to defend ourselves. Rather, it pictures us marching with confidence into the battle, completely assured of our victory over the Enemy. David's Old Testament example illustrates this New Testament principle.

7. What phrase from 1 Chronicles 14:8 reveals David's response to the Philistines' attack?

8. When you feel threatened by the Enemy—whether to engage in sin, succumb to fear, or weaken in your resolve—what is your usual response to his attack?

9. Why do you think you usually respond this way?

10. How do you think you could respond differently?

Don't misunderstand. Resisting is a term of defense rather than attack. We are not being told to go out looking for a fight but rather to feel confident in standing firmly against the threats and attacks made by our Enemy. I encourage you, sister, to stand your ground, look the Enemy in the eye, and walk in full confidence that he is already defeated and your victory already guaranteed. You do not have to succumb to the bark of this dog. Remember, there's no bite in him.

STANDING FIRM IN THE FAITH

At the time of the Philistines' attack they possessed a great advantage. They had a superior material culture that included knowledge of how to work with iron. Their advanced technology enabled them to smelt iron ore and create weaponry that the Israelites did not have. Archeological digs of sites in Israel reveal that only those occupied by Philistines contained iron tools or weapons. This iron was the "secret weapon" that would keep Israel subservient to the Philistines for centuries. The Philistines would win with crushing defeats because they had the most powerful and exact weaponry.

11. After resisting our Enemy in what are we to stand firmly planted (1 Peter 5:9)?

In David's time the Philistines may have had the secret weapon, but now we as the children of God have it (1 Pet. 5:9). We can stand firm against the Enemy's attacks because we stand on a foundation of unwavering faith and trust in the truth of God's Word.

12. This means we must know what the Scriptures declare about our standing of victory and the Enemy's standing of defeat. Faith means we act in accordance with what we know. Today begin or refresh your journey of confident faith in God's Word as your solid foundation. Copy the following Scripture verses on a note card and keep them where you can see them often. Repeat them aloud often and begin to incorporate them into your belief system.

> *"Thanks be to God, who always leads us in triumph in Christ, and manifests through us the sweet aroma of the knowledge of Him in every place" (2 Cor. 2:14, NASB).*

> *"In all these things we overwhelmingly conquer through Him who loved us" (Rom. 8:37, NASB).*

> *"Thanks be to God who gives us the victory through our Lord Jesus Christ. Therefore, my beloved brethren, be steadfast, immovable, always abounding in the work of the Lord, knowing that your toil is not in vain in the Lord" (1 Cor. 15:57-58, NASB).*

You are a victorious overcomer, completely capable by God's Spirit within you to stand against the attacks of the Enemy. Don't allow his vicious barking to cause you to run for cover. Arm yourself for battle, meet him on the field of play, and trust the Lord for your deliverance from your already-beaten foe.

13. End your day's study by repeating the Scriptures you have copied back to their author along with any other passages that have spoken to you today. Thank Him for speaking directly and personally to you through His Word.

WEEK TWO | DAY THREE
⚘ Anointed and Disappointed ⚘

"I sense that God is calling me into women's ministry as a teacher and author, but the doors to ministry aren't opening like I thought they would."—Barbara, 35

"I just got married, and my spouse and marriage are a lot different than I thought they would be. I don't feel like I can handle either one."—Amiee, 27

"I was certain that the promotion from supervisor to manager was going to be mine this time, but I've been passed over … again. I don't understand why the Lord won't allow me to have this success in my career that I've worked so hard for."—Tammy, 43

"I've always wanted children, but the doctor says that I will not be able to. Although I know God can override the doctor's prognosis, I don't know if I can live with my reality in the chance that He chooses not to."—Ebony, 31

"There aren't enough resources for me to attend the school of my choice. I have to go to a community college that doesn't offer me the same opportunities. How will I ever be the best in my field when this education is so limited?"—Karly, 19

"I've always wanted to be a doctor. I cut my education short with the birth of my first child. When the second one was born with a disability, it was put on hold again. That was 10 years ago. Now I am taking care of aging parents and it looks like my dream will never come true."—Emma, 39

"I've always felt called to be a wife and mother. It's been the longing of my heart since I was little. Homemaking is my greatest aspiration. Will I ever get married?"—Veronica, 39

My heart breaks when I read the e-mails and letters of disillusioned and frustrated women whose lives, in their estimation, seem far from the abundance and anointing they expected. I guess I can relate because in many seasons, mine has as well. While we have received Christ as Savior and know that His anointing lives in us, we can easily become discouraged when our experience doesn't read like any story line we would write for ourselves. How do we cope when what we believe God has called and anointed us to do seems to elude us?

1. If you were writing me a letter about frustration with what God has allowed in your life, what would be its main focus?

ANOINTED FOR TODAY

According to the time line of David's life on page 14, he was anointed by Samuel to be king 22 years before he actually assumed the position. Twenty-two years is a long time. I'm sure my faith would have wavered, especially when my circumstances seemed anything but empowered by God. What must David's brothers have thought during this time? Do you suppose they taunted him? How do you think David felt?

2. **Recall a time (maybe it is right now) when you questioned God's anointing in you. What circumstances caused your frustration?**

   How did you deal with it?

What a privilege it must have been for Jesse to have the king anointed from his own sons. David was so insignificant that his own father didn't even suggest him as a possibility, and yet he was the one God chose to reign as king. What happened in David's life after this anointing was most assuredly an interesting turn of events for all involved.

3. **What was David's job when he was anointed king (1 Sam. 16:11)?**

4. **What was David's job directly after he was anointed king (1 Sam. 16:17-19,21)?**

5. **What did David do between tending sheep and attending to Saul (1 Sam. 17:15,17-18)?**

6. **What significant spiritual principle do you see in the progression of David's jobs during this time?**

7. **Since you have sensed God's call on you, what has been the progression of your life?**

   * **I've felt disappointed in what the Lord has allowed to transpire.**
   * **I've felt frustrated in what the Lord has allowed to transpire.**
   * **I've felt accepting of what the Lord has allowed to transpire.**

   Why?

In the months immediately following David's anointing, God orchestrated a shocking series of events. Instead of promotion to the position of king, David submitted to serving the one already in that position. Fully aware that God's Spirit was with him to lead God's chosen people, David served in full submission as a mere armor bearer to the king. The first step after being anointed was to serve. Often servanthood and submission mark the truest test of the anointed person. David was no less anointed by God when serving than later when he sat on the throne.

8. Why do you think we often feel less spiritual/anointed/empowered by God when we are doing something that seems menial?

9. What does Luke 22:26 suggest about greatness?

10. If God asked you to serve someone who is in a position you desire, would you be willing?
   * Yes, I would love to!   * If I had to
   * I'm not sure.   * Not in a million years

   Explain your answer.

David's anointing was not merely to lead the Hebrews 22 years later. That same anointing was to empower him to walk the road to his destination and fulfill each obligation along the way. God empowered him not just to rule as king but to have patience until he sat on the throne, to submit to authority, to serve, and to have faith in God's promise despite circumstances.

What was true for David is true for you. Whatever your life entails right now—no matter how far removed it seems from what you expected—He has anointed you and divinely equipped you to not merely handle it but to thrive in it. If you can't be faithful in a little, God will not give you the larger assignment. He may want to adjust your life and character in smaller assignments to prepare you for the larger ones.[2]

"Because we know that this extraordinary day is just ahead, we pray for you all the time—pray that our God will make you fit for what he's called you to be, pray that he'll fill your good ideas and acts of faith with his own energy so that it all amounts to something. If your life honors the name of Jesus, he will honor you. Grace is behind and through all of this, our God giving himself freely, the Master, Jesus Christ, giving himself freely" (2 Thess. 1:11-12, The Message).

Carla illustrates this principle to me every day. She has worked with my husband and me at Going Beyond Ministries for two years. We met four years ago when I posted a job at Dallas Theological Seminary for a student to help this struggling mother of two toddlers for six hours a week with some of the demands of daily life. She answered the ad to make a few extra dollars while she finished her Masters in Theology degree.

After she received her diploma we said a tearful good-bye as she went on to pursue her goal of working in full-time ministry. For a year she searched for a position but found nothing. She became discouraged and frustrated as one door after another closed for her. While she prayed for God's job for her, Jerry and I were praying for the right administrative assistant for our ministry. Like a lightning bolt from heaven, Carla's name came to our minds. We approached her with the opportunity and the partnership began. This job she faithfully performs day after day is well beneath her skills and abilities. As a woman with a degree in theology who has a gift and desire to study, share, and apply God's Word in practical ways to women's lives, she has served us just as David served Saul.

She's the first to admit that administration is neither her skill set nor her desire, yet she answers phones, files papers, answers e-mails, and handles all administrative tasks without complaint. And since she works so closely with our family, she often ends up doing tasks like blowing little noses and washing a dish or two. Despite the glaring disparity between her ultimate goals and what she now does, she assumes that God's anointing on her life is not just for what might come tomorrow but is also for her life today. So she works with all her might, heartily as unto the Lord.

11. Name two people who have stories like Carla's.

What are some specific attributes that characterize these people?

EQUIPPED FOR TOMORROW WHILE ENGAGING IN TODAY

During the 22 years of waiting, we don't find David longing to be king or looking for ways to rush God's timing. Even when his life was in danger at the hands of Saul, he did not wish the worst on his enemy. Instead, he continued to trust in God's best for his life and fully commit to whatever God asked of him. In fact, David's commitment to engage in what God brought into his life was precisely what equipped him for the next set of circumstances he would face. His willingness to submit to the roll of "delivery boy" for his brothers on the battlefield led him face-to-face with Goliath (17:23). David declared his preparedness to face the giant because he had faced lions and bears (17:34-36). Each circumstance David faced and overcame strengthened him to handle the next challenge. All of those years of service were not a waste after all. Each season was a necessary part of his development to be king.

12. For what did you once wait that God has allowed to come to pass?

As you look back, what circumstances did God use to equip you to handle it?

13. Serving can become the very building block for our empowerment and development. In what ways can you plan to serve those who are presently doing what you want God to allow you to do?

Today I want to encourage you to commit your whole life to the Lord, especially if it looks drastically different than what you had in mind. Don't despair and become frustrated in the seasons of waiting that the Lord might allow you go through. Rather, ask Him to allow your spiritual eyes to clearly see His hand in every aspect of each season. Fully engage and rely on His Spirit to empower you to do what He has called you to do.

14. Spend some time in prayer. Be vulnerable about your frustrations and disappointments. Ask the Father to empower you with patience and faithfulness by His Spirit so that you can learn what He desires to teach you in every season.

WEEK TWO | DAY FOUR

The Benefits of the Anointing

Jaye Martin is a mother who lives in Houston. When I met her, I was captured as she shared the story of a store that opened near her child's elementary school. The shop was known for selling merchandise connected to the occult. She and others in the community were fairly certain that drugs were being sold there.

Jaye was a part of a mom's prayer group that began to pray for the protection of their children who spent much of their day close to the store. When they found out that some children were wandering over after school and becoming interested in all of the weird things they offered, Jaye went to see the store owner and express her concern. He assured her there was no harm in what he was offering and otherwise ignored her. Despite her request that they find a location better suited to them and the community, they refused to leave. Undeterred, she called the leasing agent and asked him to reconsider the lease because the elementary school was so close. He said that he didn't see a reason not to allow them to rent space from him. Jaye, fed up with the obvious spiritual opposition, replied matter-of-factly, "Well then, we will just have to pray them out!" The agent laughed in her face.

At her next meeting she introduced the concept of not just praying for their children's safety but praying the store out of the neighborhood. Honestly, the other mothers were stunned at this thought. Using prayer as a direct weapon was a new concept for many of them, but they prayed fervently that heaven would intervene on their behalf. Two months later, the cult store was gone.

1. **Record the details of a prayer that has made a huge impact in your life or in the life of someone you know. Prepare to share these details with your group.**

THE EAR OF GOD

In the face of immense opposition, David confidently faced his foes. Like the modern-day example of a Houston mother, he did not shrink back in fear as the enemy advanced on his territory; rather, he lunged forward in full assurance of victory. First Chronicles 14 does not give us specifics of David's primary military actions, but 2 Samuel 6 does.

2. **Record David's actions in 2 Samuel 5:17.**

According to your video lesson this week, what did David's action reveal about his chosen method of battle?

Our culture's teaching flies in the face of David's military strategy for defeating the Philistines. While he chose to seek the Lord in silence and solitude before making another move, culture teaches us to fight fast, hard, and furious. Our society encourages activity and busyness, especially when it appears that specific action is required. I admit to falling into this line of thinking. I've had to fight tooth and nail to pluck myself off of the cycle of doing before seeking.

Bent toward impatience, I am always ready to move to the next thing and often feel frustrated when I'm made to be still before making a decision. Yet I've seen others who do what David did—take time to quietly seek direction. I envy their peace in the midst of trial and their ability to make keen decisions with deep spiritual insight and wisdom.

Many today would consider these rare individuals weak and indecisive. To the contrary, David's example shows us his strength. He determined that the wisest thing he could do was to spend time seeking God's direction. One of the most incredible benefits of having God's Spirit is access to the ear of God.

3. **When you face a situation that calls for action, do you normally (check all that apply):**
   ❏ *Seek the advice of friends; then act*   ❏ *Seek God and act*
   ❏ *Seek the advice of friends, seek God; then act.*   ❏ *Seek God, wait for His direction; then act.*
   ❏ *Act immediately and then regret your actions*   ❏ *Other:*

Why wouldn't we take advantage of having the ear of God turned in our direction? Only if we believe He's not listening or if we don't believe He has the ability and desire to assist us in time of need. If we truly believed the great God of the universe listens intently to the cry of our hearts and responds with power in our circumstances, we would never meet any circumstance without deciding to access the ear of God.

4. **What do the following verses suggest to you about God's attention and ability?**

   Micah 7:7

   Isaiah 59:1-2

> *"I'll give you words and wisdom that will reduce all accusers to*
> *stammers and stutters" (Luke 21:15, The Message.)*

> *"If you don't know what you're doing, pray to the Father. He loves to help. You'll get*
> *his help, and won't be condescended to when you ask for it. Ask boldly, believingly,*
> *without a second thought. People who 'worry their prayers' are like wind-*
> *whipped waves. Don't think you're going to get anything from the Master that*
> *way, adrift at sea, keeping all your options open" (Jas. 1:5-8, The Message).*

Jesus saw the importance of seeking God before making major decisions. Jesus faced many people, including His own disciples, who were looking for Him, seeking His intervention, and demanding His time and attention. With so many opportunities I'd feel pressured to start working my way through the "to-do" list in hopes of finishing before sundown. Jesus chose another option:

"In the early morning, while it was still dark, Jesus got up, left the house, and went away to a secluded place, and was praying there" (Mark 1:35, NASB).

When the disciples found Jesus, they scolded Him for being tucked away alone while so many demands required His attention. They urged Him to engage immediately in the day's activities. Jesus' response shows His strong resolve to follow His Father instead of the pressure of His peers.

5. What does Mark 1:38 reveal about how Jesus:

Responded to His prayer time?

Responded to pressure from others?

Focused His attention on His Father's goals for Him instead of others'?

6. What are you facing that distracts you from seeking God?

THE MOUTH OF GOD

David sought the Father in 2 Samuel and Jesus sought the Father in Mark 1:35 because they both believed that God had something to say regarding their circumstances. They went to Him, fully anticipating that not only did they have access to the ear of God but that they also had access to the mouth of God.

Jesus prayerfully waited for His Father's instructions. Jesus had no divinely drawn blueprint or schedule. He discerned the Father's will day by day in a life of prayer and was able to resist the urgent demands of others and do what was really important for His mission.

For years I spent impotent time with God engaging in the duty of prayer while feeling as if it was a waste of my time. I told Him my problems and life concerns because that's how I'd been taught and because I truly believed that God would hear me. I didn't really believe God would answer and that I could have the privilege to hear His voice giving me direction.

Discovering that divine guidance is a benefit of the anointing has changed my life in unbelievable ways. Now I approach my time with the Lord and His written Word (*logos*), fully anticipating that He has a specific word (*rhema*) for me. And since I believe He has direction to give me, I am more willing to patiently wait for His response before moving forward.

7. **Two verses that guarantee believers the benefit of divine guidance are John 16:13 and 1 John 2:27. Record the most meaningful words from each.**

    John 16:13

    1 John 2:27

8. **Why do these portions speak to you?**

When the unbelievable wisdom of the apostle Paul boggled the minds of those with whom he came in contact, he answered their queries by explaining:

> *"We do speak wisdom among those who are mature; a wisdom, however, not of this age nor of the rulers of this age, who are passing away; but we speak God's wisdom in a mystery, the hidden wisdom which God predestined before the ages to our glory … For to us God revealed them through the Spirit; for the Spirit searches all things, even the depths of God. For who among men knows the thoughts of a man except the spirit of the man which is in him? Even so the thoughts of God no one knows except the Spirit of God"* (1 Cor. 2:6-7,10-11, NASB).

God speaks, and you can hear His voice. This is one of the privileges of receiving the Spirit of God.

TIME BUDGET

Most of us require discipline to carve out time to go to the stronghold and be still before God. We often think the day doesn't have enough time to do it, but really the issue is priority. Unlike money, we each have the same hours to spend each day. We all allocate those resources to what we believe is most deserving of our time. Just as we budget our finances to determine where our money should be going, it behooves us to budget our time to ensure we spend it wisely.

The best budgets begin by determining where your money currently goes and then moving to a new budget that reveals your new priorities. Think carefully about your time and work on a new budget that you can begin to follow in which spending time in the stronghold with God becomes a priority. Our success in facing the battles that life will bring depends on it.

9. **Be as detailed or as general as you like. On the next page write down how you are spending your hours.**

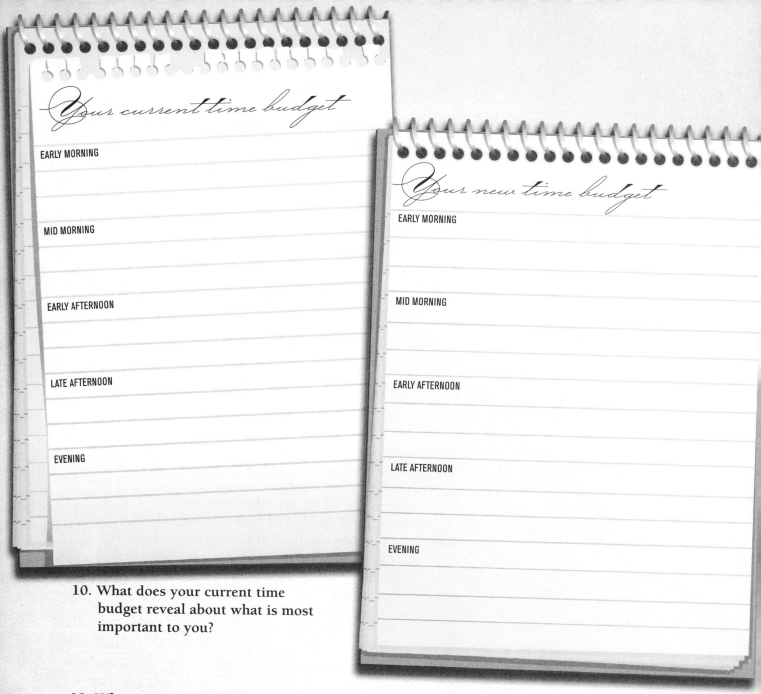

Your current time budget

EARLY MORNING

MID MORNING

EARLY AFTERNOON

LATE AFTERNOON

EVENING

Your new time budget

EARLY MORNING

MID MORNING

EARLY AFTERNOON

LATE AFTERNOON

EVENING

10. What does your current time budget reveal about what is most important to you?

11. Where can you budget some time to seek the Lord and listen for His voice?

12. Does the position of your prayer time in your new budget show that it is a priority?

13. Share your new budget goals with a friend in your group who can keep you accountable. Don't wait. Pick up the phone and call her right now.

WEEK TWO | DAY FIVE

The Responsibility of the Anointing

"And from everyone who has been given much, much shall be required; and to whom they entrusted much, of him they will ask all the more" (Luke 12:48, NASB).

I sat at the luncheon thrilled to meet with so many women from other countries and cultures involved in women's ministry. As we snacked on fruit and sandwiches, I drank in the beauty of the body of Christ represented. The myriad of accents from British to Nigerian flooded my senses and warmed my heart. When the program began, I was delighted to listen to a panel discussion where the pastor's wife hosting this event and her daughter answered questions about their lives in ministry. The questions about their personal lives and expansive ministry as a family were varied and their responses insightful, but it was what the 20-year-old daughter said that caused the spirit within me to respond with enthusiasm and conviction.

She's a bright girl who has walked with her parents along a journey in ministry from its fledgling stages to its current enormous reach. She's seen the growth, walked through the fire, and experienced the joy; now she is employed on the church's staff. When asked about the responsibility she feels to continue what God is doing, she simply said she fully recognizes the great work God has done in her parents and honors Him and them for it. Because of their faithfulness her starting place is at an entirely different place. It is hoisted securely on their shoulders. Although grateful for the positioning God had given her to work for Him and impact people, she stated somberly, "I recognize that to whom much is given, much is required." She understood that God's hand in her life wasn't just about the benefits. It also carried a weighty responsibility to hold gingerly the gifts the Lord had bestowed on her and live a life that would honor the God who gave them.

A connection always exists between benefits and responsibilities. Health insurance requires the policyholder to pay the monthly bill. The benefits of a degree require the student to complete the course work. At church, benefits of membership require a commitment to participate in ministry. We do not benefit from much on earth that does not also require a commitment to which we are held accountable. Although much of what stems from our relationship with the Father through Jesus Christ is a free gift to us, in many ways God's kingdom is no different.

BENEFITS AND RESPONSIBILITIES

God's desire to bless His children with abundance and blessing is seen from the very beginning of the Old Testament and into the church age. However, His blessing was most often tied to a requirement on the part of those He loved.

1. **According to Deuteronomy 28:1-2, what was the requirement for God's people to reap the benefits of His blessing?**

The same was true for David. As a chosen vessel, the king of Israel not only had access to the benefits of the anointing but was accountable for the responsibilities of it. His heart to pursue obedience would be the very factor that would separate his reign from that of any other king of Israel. We see this clearly in the portion of his life in 1 Chronicles 14.

2. **After seeking God and receiving directions, how did David respond to the Lord (v. 16)?**

3. **Given the instructions the Lord gave to him, why might this have been difficult (v. 15)?**

David's responsibility to the Lord was to obey even when the directions seemed less than normal. His commitment to obey shows an enormous display of trust and faith in God's abilities above his own. It is extremely difficult to obey God when His word to us is either something we don't want to hear or find difficult to obey. Yet if we desire to maintain the sweet connection of fellowship between us and the Father, remain sensitive to His Spirit, and continue to receive unfettered empowerment from Him, we must commit to obey Him.

> *"Trust in the LORD with all your heart and do not lean on your own understanding. In all your ways acknowledge Him, and He will make your path straight" (Prov. 3:5-6, NASB).*

The headline of the Life section of *USA Today* read, "Is Sin Dead?" The article, written in connection to the Easter holiday, reported on American's growing tolerance for sin and expanding lack of commitment to biblical direction. It reports a "drift of American preaching today [away from the issue of sin] in a lot of churches. People know what sin is; they just don't believe in it anymore. We mix up happiness and holiness, and God is no longer the reference point."

Only 45 percent of Americans believe sex before marriage a sin. Just over half consider homosexual activity sinful and only 63 percent think taking more change from the grocery store than you should is a sinful act.[3] Not allowing our happiness to interfere with holiness can be a difficult challenge in a culture like ours. While some have decided to skirt the issue of sin in exchange for a more gentle gospel, the Bible never does. You and I must take a staunch stand against this cultural trend away from obedience to God and His Word. We must determine to obey Him fully and completely regardless of what others may do.

4. **In today's tolerant culture, what can you do to protect your thinking and your children's thinking regarding God's view of sin?**

5. **In what areas of your life do you find obedience to be most difficult?**

6. **In the chart at the top of page 55, make a list of some current instructions God has given you that you have not yet followed through on; then list the reason why.**

_____

_____

_____

_____

When I make a list like this and look at it carefully, I see that no reason to procrastinate is a good one. For some reason what sounds good clanking around the chambers of our minds can look unbelievably ridiculous when written on paper. Is there ever a good explanation for not immediately obeying God, especially when disobedience costs us an abundantly fulfilling, empowering relationship with Him? Most of my reasons boiled down to nothing more than issues of fear, self-centeredness, or plain old rebellion. What about yours? We would do well to remember that the only alternative to obedience is disobedience. There is no middle ground.

IMPERFECT YET REPENTANT

One of the best ways to see the importance of obedience in David's life is to contrast it with the life of another. Like David, Saul was also chosen by God for leadership in Israel and had been anointed by the Spirit of God to undertake the task. Both had similar beginnings. The prophet Samuel sought them both out at God's bidding to anoint them to reign as king. But as quickly as we see the comparisons, the contrasts begin.

> *"Then Samuel said to Saul, 'Stop! Listen to what the Lord told me last night!' … Although you may think little of yourself, are you not the leader of the tribes of Israel? The Lord has anointed you king of Israel. … Why haven't you obeyed the Lord? Why did you … do what was evil in the Lord's sight?" (1 Sam. 15:16,17,19, NLT).*

Saul's reign was characterized by jealousy that ripened into murder (1 Sam. 18:8-12). He also refused to acknowledge his sin when confronted by the prophet, sought to rationalize his behavior, and made dishonest excuses (15:20-21). However, the problem with Saul was not just these imperfections (since even David had some); the main problem was that his heart was hardened toward God. Repenting and returning to the God who had anointed him was not his priority, and this is what would ultimately cause his untimely demise.

David was by no means perfect. He chose a sinful path that led to adultery and murder. Like Saul before him, he became engrossed in a tangled web of lies and murder in an attempt to escape the consequences of his actions. With a pregnant mistress at his side, he succumbed to sins grip and was strangled in its clutches. For a moment, David must have thought that he had gotten away with murder. The problem was—God saw. And so "the thing that David had done was evil in the sight of the Lord" (2 Sam. 11:27, NASB).

Recall a time when you felt as if you had gotten away with something but later discovered that God was displeased and was holding you accountable for your actions. How did your experience compare to David's? The Lord sent the prophet Nathan to David to condemn his sin. After clearly reporting God's opinion on the matter at hand, Nathan gave a clear rebuke straight from God.

7. Turn to 2 Samuel 12:7-9 (NASB) where God points out why David would be punished for His sin. Fill in the blanks below.

It is I who _____ you _____ over Israel (v. 7).

It is _____ who _____ you from the hand of _____ (v. 7).

I also gave you _____ and your _____ into your care and

I gave you the house of _____ and Judah (v. 8).

Notice David's responsibility was tied to God's gracious blessings. In the words Jesus gave to the disciples, "from everyone who has been given much, much will be required" (Luke 12:48, NASB). God even said He would have blessed David more, and yet David didn't hold up his end of the bargain. David had seen the demise of Saul and knew that God's Spirit had been removed for his disobedience to the Lord. Inevitably, this is what led him to pray that the Lord would not take His Holy Spirit from him (Ps. 51:11), and he offered sincere repentance throughout Psalm 51. By no means was David perfect, but by all accounts he was sincerely repentant. While Saul's heart was hardened, David acknowledged his sin, sought the Lord's forgiveness, and began to walk down a different path.

Where do you stand between the two extremes of David and Saul? Though we are all imperfect, does your response to God's conviction most closely mirror David's or Saul's? Although we can never lose the Spirit's presence as Old Testament saints could, it is possible to "grieve the Holy Spirit" (Eph. 4:30), vex the Spirit (Isa. 63:10), and see His potency in your life quenched (1 Thess. 5:19). Are you and I determined to be responsible carriers of God's Spirit and make every attempt to be certain that He is never grieved? Our commitment to this will determine our continued level of supernatural ability to accomplish God's purposes in our existence.

> *"And the Spirit of the LORD came mightily upon David from that day forward. …*
> *Now the Spirit of the LORD departed from Saul" (1 Sam. 16:13-14, NASB).*

8. Record the main principles you have learned from David's story in 1 Chronicles 14 in the past two weeks. How have these impacted your life?

Thank you for sharing the last two weeks with me. It has been such an honor to walk with you through one small portion of David's incredible journey. Ask the Spirit to cause what He's already taught you to become a building block for what you are about to learn in the upcoming weeks of this study. Sister, hold on to your hat. That incredible Bible-teaching tornado Miss Beth is up next. I've already worked through her lessons and listened to her messages and I know that God is going to speak to you in a way you will never forget.

1. Chuck Swindoll. *Flying Closer to the Flame* (Nashville, TN: Thomas Nelson, 1995), 246-247.

2. Henry T. Blackaby and Claude V. King. *Experiencing God* (Nashville, TN: LifeWay Press, 1990), 39.

3. Cathy Lynn Grossman. "Has the 'notion of sin' been lost?" *USA Today* [online], 20 March 2008 [cited 22 April 2008].

Available from the Internet: *http://www.usatoday.com/news/religion/2008-03-19-sin_N.htm?loc=interstitialskip*

BETHMOORE

TRANSFORMED

VIEWERGUIDE

MOVING PAST OUR DEVASTATION

1. We can have a _____ idea that's not a _____ idea (Luke 2:4).

2. _____ _____ moments with God

3. There's a very big difference between _____ and _____.

4. God has come to absolutely mark our lives with His glory. … He's come to take us _____ _____. … So far it has to be God.

5. God is not interested in just adjusting our lives. He wants us _____.

6. I don't want a tweak; I want a transformation. … A full-fledged _____ _____ transformation.

7. What will it take to get there?

8. We've got to move past our _____ with God (2 Sam. 6:1-10).

   David was …

   • _____ (v. 8)

   • _____ (v. 9)

Group Discussion Questions

1. Looking back over your life since you became a Christian, what is one area in which you have grown?

2. Has God taken you anywhere that you never thought you would go? If so, where?

3. What has been the most surprising aspect of your relationship with God? What has been the most treasured part of that relationship to you?

WEEK THREE | DAY ONE

Something for You

"Here I am, living in a palace of cedar, while the ark of God remains in a tent"
(2 Sam. 7:2, NIV).

Hey, Dear One! I am so honored to serve you alongside my good friends, Priscilla and Kay. This is my first opportunity to be part of a team of teachers in a written Bible study series, and I could not respect either of them more.

The concept for this series is a vivid reflection of how we each feel. We don't want women in Bible study camps. We want them in the Bible! We don't want them to become followers of a teacher. We want them to be followers of Christ! Thank you so much for giving us the joy of washing your feet in the water of God's Word and giving us the freedom to serve you in our own styles.

I pray that the love we share for Scripture is an encouragement to you, but equally I ask God to make our differences a blessing. Our infinitely creative God orders each of our lives to be as unique as our DNA. As He develops you in your own gifts and calling, by all means take direction from others you respect, but resist trying to imitate their distinctions. To do so is to forfeit your own. A proactive way to cooperate with God while He makes you a one-of-a-kind expression of Christ is to intentionally place yourself under the influence of many teachers. You will end up becoming a wonderfully unique concoction of all those godly influences. Let me see if I can explain.

Six primary servants of God had profound influences on my life in the strategic years God poured the foundation for this ministry. At one time I felt pressured to be just like them but, then again, I'd ask myself, Which one? When all was said and done, I developed into someone different from each of them because, metaphorically speaking, I was a blend of all of them. Add to the mix a heaping helping of my own God-given personality and the result is someone distinct. Weird, yes. But distinct. Make sense? Perhaps you know exactly what I mean because you've developed similarly.

1. **Name several people God has used to make the biggest investments on the servant you are becoming in Christ. Beside each name, write a phrase describing what you've received most from that person.**

_____ : _____

_____ : _____

_____ : _____

_____ : _____

_____ : _____

Now go back and draw a "+" under each line to add it to the next. Then, in the space under the last line, jot down several ways you are distinct from all of them. The sum total is a tiny glimpse of who you are.

Your uniqueness as an earthen vessel of Christ in your generation will often result from having a couple of tablespoons of one person's influence in you, a fourth of a cup of another's, and a teaspoon of many. Thank you for taking the lid off your own vessel and allowing Priscilla, Kay, and me to pour in a few things. None of us takes the privilege lightly. Among many other things, I pray that this unique format of three teachers makes a sizable investment in your own distinctiveness as a servant of God.

Throughout this week and next, we will reflect and expound on the material that we share in the sessions. For God to use this material most profoundly in your life, you don't just need to listen. You need a chance to respond and a format to explore what God is saying specifically to you. This is where a lecture becomes a discussion and an impression works its way into an expression.

In weeks 3 and 4 I'll walk you back through important parts of our sessions, develop them further, and give you a chance to reflect, respond, and receive. With that approach in mind, let's turn back to the verses that launched this session.

2. Please read 2 Samuel 7: 1-17 and answer the following questions:

According to verse 2, why was David uncomfortable living in a palace?

What advice did the prophet Nathan give to David (v. 3)?

The verses that follow indicate to us that Nathan's initial counsel to David was hasty. He assumed something that is not always true. Just because the Lord was with David didn't mean he should go ahead and do whatever he had in mind. He was still flesh and blood. His ways were not always God's ways nor were his thoughts always God's thoughts (Isa. 55:9). His heart was right, but his remedy wasn't.

As surely as the Lord was with David, He is with you and me. The first advent of Christ hailed Him as Emmanuel, the God who is with us, and His Spirit dwells inside believers. I have learned the hard way, however, that not every good idea is a God-idea. This workbook doesn't have the space to record all the great ideas I've tried and failed to implement because they simply weren't God's will.

3. What was your last good idea that turned out not to be a God-idea?

   What emotions did you go through associated with the situation?

   What has God taught you through the circumstance?

   Do you feel like you're still carrying some scars from God saying no to your plans?

Some of our examples are funny, but some still hit a nerve and make us want to cry. The disappointment and confusion lingers. Sometimes we reflect on times we tried to do something right and do it well and still think to ourselves, It should have worked! God just decided not to bless it! Today's lesson gives us the perfect opportunity to let God heal a few lingering wounds.

Just because David confused a good idea with a God-idea didn't mean he had failed. God could see straight into his heart and was well acquainted with his motive. God can also bless our lives profoundly for our pure-hearted plans even when He can't, for kingdom reasons, bless our idea.

4. Take great note of God's message back to David. What did the Lord "declare" to him in the latter part of verse 11?

Do you see it? When David wanted to build a house for God, He responded, "You're not going to build a house for Me. I'm going to build a house for you!" As we conclude today's lesson, take this personally: When God doesn't appear to bless your plan to do something for Him, consider that He wants to do something for you instead. Ask Him what! Then, as He reveals it to you over time, cooperate and let Him do it! Every work of our hands that God truly blesses always originates with a specific work of His in us.

Listen, Beloved. You aren't—nor have you ever been—a failure. Anything God has stopped you from doing for Him was only so you'd be still enough to let Him first do something for you.

WEEK THREE | DAY TWO

Getting This Far

*"Who am I, O Sovereign LORD, and what is my family, that you
have brought me this far?" (2 Sam. 7:18, NIV).*

In our previous lesson we reflected on God's message to David through the prophet Nathan.
You'll recall that David was unsettled by the absurdity that he had a palace while the ark of the
covenant rested in a tent.

**1. David's solution was to build a fitting house for the ark, but God had something different
in mind. What was it?**

Theologians appropriately call God's promises to David the Davidic Covenant. It represents
a confirmation and expansion of the original Abrahamic Covenant in Genesis 12. The most
significant part of the Davidic Covenant culminates in the New Testament.

2. Read Luke 2:4-11 and record each reference to David.

Christ Jesus was the point and will be the culmination of every covenant of God in Scripture.
"For no matter how many promises God has made, they are 'Yes' in Christ. And so through him
the 'Amen' is spoken by us to the glory of God" (2 Cor. 1:20). May His great name be praised!

Today we'll look at David's response to God's insistence on first building a "house" for Him. We'll
fasten our gaze to the passage that became our theme in session 3; then we will expound on it.

3. Read 2 Samuel 7:18-20. What question pierced David's tender heart?

**Have you ever come to a time in your life when you asked the same question?
If so, describe the circumstances.**

TRANSFORMED

Few words coming from the mouth of flesh and blood in Scripture move me more than these. David voiced the sentiment of countless followers of God who have been startled by His scandalous grace through the centuries. I am one of them.

Who, indeed, am I, O Lord? And who is my family that you have brought us this far? Keith and I were like two wrecked cars that sped frantically through a red light and had a head-on collision. One colossal wreck made up of two.

Recently I met a young man who'd taken over the position as administrator of a well-known Texas hill-country retreat center. He told me how loved the previous administrator had been and how he'd just retired. Hearing the retiree's very unusual name set my heart ablaze with memories. He served as the counselor at a church in Houston 29 years ago and counseled Keith and me in our very early and troubled marriage. I said to my new friend, "Would you please tell him that Keith and Beth Moore made it? You'll have to insist because he won't believe it!"

In session 3 we talked about allowing God to bring us "so far" that He alone could be the excuse for it. We talked about becoming the person only God could make us. We talked about not just feeling better but being freed. Not just being relieved but being released. Not just being adjusted but transformed. Not just being delayed in our trip to the next pit but completely delivered.

You and I don't want to stop cooperating with God until He has accomplished a wonder-driven work that has taken us "so far" that He gets profuse credit. All of us are in process, so don't let yourself slip into an inch of condemnation as we explore some distance we've come. My reason for probing is to prompt you to give God enormous praise if you've already experienced a "so far" kind of work and, if you haven't, to plead with you not to settle for anything less.

3. To the best of your understanding, try to plot where you believe you might be in your progress toward a work "so far" that only God can be the explanation:

| Can't see any progress | A little progress | Significant progress | Come so far! |

Throughout the remainder of weeks 3 and 4 we're going to discuss some obstacles to a "so far" work that we can start shoving out of the way immediately. For the remainder of our lesson today, however, let's focus on a very specific dimension of David's response to God. He was awe-stricken not only about how far God had brought him but he was also floored by what God had done for his family.

If you're like me, you don't just want a "so far" work for yourself. You want it for your loved ones! In session 3 I asked you to begin voraciously praying that God would accomplish a "so far" kind of work throughout your entire family. I also recommended that you compile a list of 10 or so Scriptures you could begin praying for them with confidence.

I don't always pray using Scripture, but if the request is serious and the length of time sustained, I turn to this method every time. Somehow, if I'm using Scripture, I can more easily shift the burden over to God and His Word in matters that are most wearying and faith challenging.

4. Please look up the following passages of Scripture and reword them into prayers for your family or a specific loved one. While you're at it, don't forget to pray them for yourself! This exercise will take a few minutes, but the effectiveness you can gain in prayer will be inconceivably worth it. I've even given you a chance to add other Scripture that the Lord brings to mind.

Psalm 18:16-19   Dear Father in heaven, in accordance with Your powerful, life-giving Word, I ask You …

Proverbs 2:7-8   Dear Father in heaven, in accordance with Your powerful, life-giving Word, I ask You …

Proverbs 4:23-27   Dear Father in heaven, in accordance with Your powerful, life-giving Word, I ask You …

Romans 12:1-2   Dear Father in heaven, in accordance with Your powerful, life-giving Word, I ask You …

_____   Dear Father in heaven, in accordance with Your powerful, life-giving Word, I ask You …

_____   Dear Father in heaven, in accordance with Your powerful, life-giving Word, I ask You …

Beloved, keep a copy of the previous page with your Bible so you can have it handy during your prayer time. Read it regularly (and aloud when possible) as intercession before the throne of grace and with absolute confidence in what you're asking. It's God's Word! Use these for several weeks. When you can tell you're losing some of your freshness with them, ask God to equip you with new ones.

5. John 15:7-8 continues to be one of my primary inspirations to let God's Word abide in me and then turn into powerful intercession for myself and for others. In your own words, what did Christ tell His followers in these two verses?

No one bats .1000 in prayer, but, make no mistake, Christ meant for our prayer lives to have explosive power and effectiveness. I believe these two verses coupled together indicate that one primary way our lives bear much fruit is through learning to pray according to God's will and then, glory to His name, receiving what we asked!

This is the connection between abiding words and effective prayers:

The words of Christ forms ⟶ the will of Christ, and ⟶ we grow exponentially in receiving what we ask.

The result is a life that bears much fruit. I want that kind of life, and I think you do too.

Please seek God for other Scriptures that you can turn into intercession for your family's progress, in addition to the ones I've supplied. Pray, pray, pray until you can say, with face-to-the-ground astonishment and thanksgiving, "Who am I, O Sovereign LORD, and what is my family that You have brought us THIS FAR?" Then pray some more.

I love you, Dear One. Great job today!

WEEK THREE | DAY THREE
~ Angry and Afraid ~

"David was afraid of the Lord that day and said, 'How can the ark of the Lord ever come to me?' " (2 Sam. 6:9, NIV).

The focus of our two weeks of study together is to determine how we can allow God to take us and our families "so far" that He alone can be the explanation. In session 3 I presented the question like this: "What can we do to cooperate with God so that He can do a rip-roaring work that alters an entire family line? How can people like you and me experience a 'this far' work of God?" Before launching into three specific answers conveyed through David's example, we talked about the crucial role of prayer toward a titanic work of God. Yesterday' we compiled Scriptures we can turn into powerful intercession for our families and ourselves. I hope you've already begun to use them confidently in prayer.

Today we will recall and expound on the first of three ways we can cooperate with God so that He can take us far beyond anything we could've imagined: We've got to move past our devastation with God.

Let's review the text supporting this statement from session 3, but this time slowly enough to respond to it.

1. **Please rewind the clock on David's life to 2 Samuel 6 and read verses 1-11. Had a *Jerusalem Chronicle* existed at that time, what do you think the headline would have been for the top story in the next morning's paper?**

2. **What did David and 30 thousand men set out to do? Choose one.**
   * rebuild the tabernacle   * subdue the remaining enemies
   * rebuild the city of Jerusalem   * bring the ark to Jerusalem

3. **According to verse 3 how did they transport the sacred vessel?**

4. **What were David and "the whole house of Israel" doing as the ark was being transported? Choose one.**
   * celebrating with all their might   * falling prostrate before God
   * offering sacrifices to God   * proclaiming the Word of God

5. Scripture records two emotions David felt toward God after Uzzah was killed. What were they? _____ and _____

6. How could the ark have such devastating effects on Uzzah and such blessing on the household of Obed-edom? Offer your thoughts.

In our session we touched on the traumatic complication of experiencing devastation at a time of expected celebration. Now let's pounce on it. Uzzah's death would have been shocking under the most somber of circumstances, but imagine the emotional whiplash David experienced when cheers turned dramatically to wails and a parade turned into pall bearing.

All of us, to varying degrees, have taken an unexpected, uninvited emotional dive, but some have endured the unimaginable. When I was in Alaska a few years ago, I learned of a young couple who were killed in a small aircraft as they traveled a brief distance from their wedding to their honeymoon destination. I tried to imagine the emotional plummet of those two sets of happy parents. The prospect alone nearly ruined my trip.

A few days before Christmas my young-adult friend Stephanie was her way home to spend the holidays with her mother. A truck fishtailed on the winter ice, and my friend spent Christmas in heaven instead. Perhaps all of us have known couples joyfully expecting a baby only to learn that something undeterminable had happened in the womb and a heartbeat could no longer be found. I could cry writing the words, especially because I know that someone reading this has endured it. I am so, so sorry for your pain.

We could list other less traumatic examples that still caused considerable emotional whiplash. I have a friend who was told he was being considered for a promotion, but when his boss called him into his office, he was laid off instead. Devastation always involves heartbreak, but a heart dropped from 90 feet shatters, splinters, and scatters differently than the one dropped from 10 feet. Devastation that should have been celebration is almost more than we can take. We are simply and understandably unprepared.

7. When have you seen or experienced the kind of emotional plummeting I've just described?

It's horrible, isn't it? At times like those, we're so dumbstruck that all we can do is throw our hand over our mouth like Job (Job 40:4). Words fail, but far more consequentially, faith often fails.

Nothing has the capacity to cause more destruction in a believer's life than an occurrence that makes us question everything we thought we knew about God. A heart can shatter in so many pieces that we don't think even God could put it back together again. If I may be so bold, sometimes we're so upset with Him we feel like we wouldn't let Him if He tried. Sometimes we halt our progress and refuse restoration just to spite Him.

I'm squirming over the subject matter too, but I've seen too many high-potential lives at a dead stop not to address the cause. God searches and knows every emotion and reaction we harbor all the way down to our deepest resentments and indicting questions. He longs to be gracious to us and restore us with His unwavering love.

We can spend decades refusing to budge an inch with God because something happened that we couldn't reconcile with our assumptions. The cross of Christ stretched out across all humanity and won a "this far" work for every person who puts her trust in Him. However, we can choose to remain right where we are for the rest of our lives. Every inch of ground we refuse to take with God, we surrender to the enemy. Satan has no greater agenda than to talk you and me into believing that God is not good after all.

8. **Take another look at the two emotions David felt toward God in 2 Samuel 6:8-9. Have you ever felt one or both of these emotions toward God? If so, when?**

David felt anger and fear toward God, yet Scripture calls him "a man after God's own heart." Neither emotion was his last feeling. For David, both were means of reacting to and working through a tragedy on his willing way to remedy.

We must not let anger or fear be our last feeling on a matter either. Neither can be sustained in our systems without turning to poison. Satan has too much to gain by your hanging onto them. You and your family have too much to lose.

Accepting the challenge to work through crisis and conflict can be a tremendously important part of developing closeness in a relationship. Don't deny it. Don't work around it. Don't back up from it. Work right through the middle of it with your God. He has never left you. Never ceased loving you. And never shut off His goodness from you.

9. **Psalm 136:1 records two of the most repetitive statements about God in all Scripture. What are they?**

10. **How many times does this one psalm voice those two statements? _____**

Those exact words are proclaimed numerous other times but in terms of our present subject matter none more significantly than 1 Chronicles 16:34. There David proclaimed them as praise to his faithful God not long after the events that took Uzzah's life. He found his heart, healed and restored, at home again with God and the ark at home again in Jerusalem. Remember, David's awed moment with God over how far He'd brought him came after the nightmare with the ark.

God has so far to take you and your family. In the depths of your heart, you don't really want to spend the rest of your life angry, afraid, and in the same old place, do you? Would you begin today by simply telling Him that you're willing to step forward with Him even if you don't have all the answers? His hand is outstretched. His heart is unleashed.

WEEK THREE | DAY FOUR

A Safe Place to Move On

*"Trust in him at all times, O people; pour out your hearts
to him, for God is our refuge" (Ps. 62:8, NIV).*

We're dealing with a very uncomfortable subject: feeling anger and the unhealthy fear toward God over an experience of devastation. I don't know if I could have even taught on this subject 15 years ago. I might have been scared half to death of getting hit by lightening for inciting the ire of God, but I've come to love Him and trust Him so much more since then.

I've also spent a little time studying the rapport of servants such as David, Job, Jeremiah, and Paul with our same God. Their relationships were like springs of living waters coming from very deep wells. Through their examples, I've become convinced that we are safe both to bring the heights of our ecstatic joys to God and find company and to bring Him the depths of our ugliest emotions and find healing.

Acting like we feel something we don't is not piety. It is pretense. It is dishonesty. Sometimes it's even hypocrisy, dishonesty at its ugliest. True intimacy cannot grow in an untrue environment. God looks straight at the heart and is more deeply acquainted with all we feel than we are. Psalm 44:21 tells us He "knows the secrets of the heart." In fact, He understands not only what we feel in those secret places but why we feel it.

Never in a hundred years would I recommend disrespect with God, but I wouldn't recommend dishonesty either. The following Scriptures demonstrate some of the balance.

1. Look up each Scripture and paraphrase it below:

   Psalm 62:8

   Psalm 109:21-22

   Psalm 145:18

We'll have a mighty tough time getting over feelings we don't feel safe enough to voice to God. If you're like me, you often can't even reach the tender feelings you have until you've dealt with the troubled ones.

I remember confessing to God one time in prayer that I absolutely hated a particular person. In fact, I said it over and over in those turbulent moments with God until I began to sob and get down to the truth of the matter: She'd hurt my feelings terribly. But, no, in actuality, I didn't hate her. Had I not felt the freedom to pour out the toxic part of my heart, I would never have reached the tenderness, crying it out enough to realize that I didn't hate her after all.

2. Have you ever experienced anything similar with God? If so, explain.

Much healing came to me that day. It was honest emotion that I never shared with another soul because I knew it would cause someone to stumble. God, however, never trips over my admissions. He knew something more and began in that moment to slather me with the healing balm of His Spirit.

Our hearts never need pouring out more than when they're filled with the toxic waters of bitterness. David, the psalmist, knew that the lifeblood of a relationship with God was constant and conscious openness to His love, His presence, and His restoration.

In all likelihood, the death of Uzzah in 2 Samuel 6 and the eruption of emotions it caused were terrifying to David. After the depth of relationship he'd shared with God and a love that he'd testified was "better than life," he surely knew he stood at a critical point in his journey. David could either sit down in the dirt, throw a handful on his head, and refuse to get up or he could pour his heart out, bawl his eyes out, catch his God-given breath, and cling to Him for dear life.

At times in our lives we will have the same two options. Sometimes we arrive at a place where we can either lose or gain ground, but returning to life as it was before is no longer an option. Change has stormed the gate. We will decide over the days and months to come if it will be positive or negative and whether we will glorify God or, Lord help us, vilify Him.

Beloved, God's ways will always be higher than ours, but we don't have to understand Him to settle the matter in our hearts that we can trust Him. At times when I've been most baffled by something that God in His sovereignty has permitted, I've reflected—often with tears streaming down my cheeks—on the interchange between Christ and His disciples in John 6:66-69.

3. Read John 6:66-69. What question did Christ ask?

4. What was Peter's response to the question?

Even in my times of greatest confusion I could not imagine ever doing anything but living life with Jesus. To whom would I go when Jesus alone has the words of life? I've lived on those words. Survived on them! The entire hard drive of my mind has been rewired by them.

What about the One who speaks them? I've enjoyed Him so! Laughed with Him. Cried with Him. Sought Him. Found refuge in Him. Bathed in His unwavering love. I've discovered His ways to be right even when they force me to die to my own screaming flesh.

Jesus is the essence of spiritual, mental, and emotional health. He is wholesomeness. He is healing. Even without all the answers to my questions, He is the answer to my life. He is my wandering soul's truest quest. I cannot imagine ever leaving His side, scarred for me, even when my heart is broken by something I think He could have stopped. Should have stopped. Even if I tried to back away, He will not budge from me.

5. What about you, Beloved? What have you found at Jesus' side that distancing yourself from Him at a time of devastation could jeopardize?

6. Read 2 Samuel 6:9-12 and explore the intriguing turning point in the saga of David and his disastrous attempt to bring the ark to Jerusalem. How did his anger and fear begin turning back to joy?

7. What did David find out in verse 12?

I'm not sure we'll glean more insight into David's heart for God than in this subtle implication. Stay with me here. When David learned how God blessed the house of Obed-edom, his hope returned and his joy soon followed. So, what's the big deal?

The blessings over the other man's household reminded the man after God's own heart that God was good and faithful. He could have had an altogether different reaction to the news. Had David not had such a heart for God, he could have been jealous, bitter, and flooded with resentment. Few things will test our hearts more thoroughly than God's shameless blessing over other lives when we're enduring a time of hardship and perhaps chastisement.

Reflect on a time when you watched God richly bless someone else in an area of finances, ministry, physical healing, or the like while you were enduring something painful. Picture him or her as your own version of Obed-edom. How did you respond to it? Before you answer the question, please trust that the purpose is not to make you feel condemned if you didn't handle it well. Rather, it is to help us see if we've distanced ourselves from God and grown resentful so we can then run back home to His heart.

8. What was your response to God's blessing someone while you were in pain?

In session 4 we're going to talk about John the Baptist and his confusion over why Jesus, with all His power and authority, allowed His own relative and forerunner to sit in jail while He was performing numerous miracles elsewhere. Let's give the segment an advance look to deepen the impact when we reach it in the session.

9. Read Luke 7:18-23. While John the Baptist sat in jail, what specific works did Christ accomplish for many others?

Christ's statement will become highly important to us over our two weeks of study together: "Blessed is the man who does not fall away on account of me!" (v. 23). The New King James rendering is particularly poignant: "Blessed is he who is not offended because of Me."

10. In similar circumstances, why might a believer become offended because of Jesus?

Not only did Jesus allow John to be imprisoned, but He also allowed him to be executed. Beheaded, for crying out loud!

John was right. Jesus did treat him differently from the masses he heard about. Jesus caused John's blind eyes to open to the very face of God.

He caused his lame legs to *dance* on golden roads.

He caused his leprous sin to be *cured* for all eternity from its hidden lusts, secret greeds, and self-righteous boasts.

The dead were indeed *raised* and the forerunner of Jesus heard the best news of all:

Welcome, My good and faithful servant!

Enter into your Master's happiness!"

Sometimes there's just a bigger plan.

WEEK THREE | DAY FIVE
The Right Kind of Fear

"David was afraid of the LORD that day and said, 'How can the ark
of the LORD ever come to me?' " (2 Sam. 6:9, NIV).

Thank you so much for staying attentive and involved through difficult subject matter. If you've endured a terrible devastation and found yourself responding negatively to God about it, my earnest prayer is that He'll use these words to open the floodgates of fresh dialogue between you so He can minister His lavish love and restoration to your soul. You are His cherished child.

As God would time it, I had an interruption between this paragraph and the last. I rarely answer the phone while I'm writing, but Keith, Amanda, or Melissa get to interrupt at will. I try never to be off limits to them and hope to have the same arrangement with my grandchildren. Thankfully, my family members try to exercise a measure of sensitivity, but the kind of closeness we're after is impossible without open accessibility. The phone call I received a few moments ago didn't even begin with a hello. It went like this: "Mom! Pray with me right now! Stephanie is on the way to the hospital this second to have her baby!"

Amanda was not upset. She was ecstatic, but she was also adamant about calling on the power and presence of God to be with a couple she has loved since high school. You see, they've already lost one child and wrestled fitfully through the emotional mine field of infertility. Amanda wants them to love Jesus and find abundant life in Him and knows that, after all they've been through, they can either become offended with Jesus or hail Him as their Deliverer, Provider, and Healer. I have a feeling you can relate as a friend to someone standing at a crossroad.

1. Have you prayed for someone you care about to draw close to God after a disaster instead of developing an offense toward Him? What were the circumstances?

2. What has been the result so far?

Amanda can't wait for her friends to behold the miracle of their darling little one, still wet and squirming and with eyes squinting from the shock of a bright light. She wants them to know the mystery of staring into the face of a precious little stranger wondrously comprised of the two of them. Amanda yearns for them to hold their baby in their arms and whisper through tears of joy, "Thank You, Jesus. Thank You!"

God is the Author of life, not man nor science. Indeed Jeremiah 1:5 says, "Before I formed you in the womb I knew you, before you were born I set you apart." The psalmist responded to a strikingly similar God-given revelation with these words:

"Certainly you made my mind and heart; you wove me together in my mother's womb. I will give you thanks because your deeds are awesome and amazing. You knew me thoroughly; my bones were not hidden from you, when I was made in secret and sewed together in the depths of the earth. Your eyes saw me when I was inside the womb. All the days ordained for me were recorded on your scroll before one of them came into existence. How difficult it is for me to fathom your thoughts about me, O God! How vast is their sum total!" (Ps. 139:13-17, NET).

We desperately need reminders like these especially when something horrible has happened. We've got to know we're cherished and have been since—take time for wonder—before we were conceived. We were planned by someone who pondered the panoramic canvas of our entire lives, in living color, dimension, and texture, with joy as if it had already been well lived. We were assigned purpose and placed within a God-created system where no pain can come to us unless it serves that exact purpose. We need to know that the events we find so baffling don't mean God has forgotten about us or forsaken us. Perhaps, if we'd stretch our hearts and minds to perceive it, He has instead trusted us.

This week in our study, we're talking about the crucial, conscious activity of moving past devastation with God so that we can proceed with God to work so titanic that we're left proclaiming, "Who am I, O Sovereign LORD, and what is my family, that you have brought me this far?"

We've been reminded how before David's great awe with God—that led him to cry out, "How great you are, O Sovereign LORD! There is no one like you!"—he first experienced the stunning, deadly failure to bring the ark into Jerusalem. Though David had been angry and afraid (2 Sam. 6:8-9), the word of God's blessing on the lives of others steeled and steadied his conviction that God is totally good. He is completely righteous. He is always holy.

David then went back for the ark and took every ounce of his shaken heart to the God he'd loved since childhood. A bruised heart that chooses to beat with a passion for God amid pulsing pain and confusion may just be the most expensive offering placed on the divine altar. He esteems yours as much as He esteemed His beloved David's.

For the last several days, we've talked about the anger David experienced over Uzzah's untimely death during the fever-pitch celebration of God's holy nation. Anger was one of two emotional responses Scripture records in reference to David.

3. Fill in the blank from 2 Samuel 6:8-9: "David was _____ that day" (v. 9).

We wrap up our third week of study centering on the fear that overcame David after the shock of Uzzah's death. If you and I are going to have relationships with God like the man after His own heart, we must distinguish between healthy and unhealthy fear of God. We can rest assured that a healthy fear of God is a beautiful thing since numerous Scriptures extol its virtues and results.

4. **The following are only a handful of them. Please read each one and record what you learn about fear of the Lord.**

Psalm 128:1

_____

Psalm 145:19

_____

Psalm 147:11

_____

Proverbs 9:10

_____

Proverbs 14:27

5. **Consider the discussion of healthy and unhealthy fear in the following four paragraphs. Underline the ideas that speak to you or that you want to remember.**

Proverbs 10:27 goes far enough to tell us, "The fear of the LORD adds length to life." Obviously, a certain kind of fear of God is healthy all right! We can, however, develop a fear toward God that is not healthy. Since the same Hebrew word for fear (lexical form: yirah) is found in both negative and positive contexts and for both appropriate and inappropriate reactions, how can we know the difference?

Consider carefully: A healthy fear of God draws us toward Him. An unhealthy fear of God draws us away from Him. A healthy fear of God bows to His holiness and obeys His precepts but all the while is compelled like a magnet to the source of its fascination. It seeks Him like hidden treasure. It stretches and strains to peer into His perfections. It yearns to be captivated by His beauty from so near a place that it becomes beautiful too. It longs to approach the One who dwells in unapproachable light. To know the unknowable till faith turns to sight. To be ruined for every other contesting love.

Unhealthy fear runs from God and recoils at the thought of trusting Him. It associates Him more with pain than praise. It sees Him as an angry god to appease rather than a wise and holy Father we need to obey but whom we can also trust. Unhealthy fear associates the glory of God solely with the agony of man. It believes that His gain always means our pain. Oh, if we could only comprehend that His gain cannot fail to also be ours, whether or not pain is involved in the worthy process.

God can never do Himself right and do His children wrong. God's glory and goodness are inseparable. (Compare Ex. 33:19,21.) We're scared to live fully surrendered to God because we're afraid it will kill us. If only we understood that any part of us crucified in doing His will becomes a hotbed of resurrection power. Where we die to self, the Spirit of Christ is raised in us.

6. **What part of the paragraphs on healthy fear versus unhealthy fear speaks most personally to you? Explain why.**

Thankfully, an unhealthy fear of God can be transformed without delay into a healthy fear of God. We see hints of this process in the man after God's own heart in 2 Samuel 6:9-12.

7. **Read these passages once again. Note that after Uzzah was killed, David was "afraid of the Lord" and was "_____ _____ to take the ark of the Lord to be with him in the City of David." (See v. 10 to fill in the blanks.)**

Subsequently, the ark remained in the house of Obed-edom for three months. For a brief time David's fear paralyzed him. He knew that the presence of God was associated with the ark of the covenant, but he was momentarily unwilling to do anything further to draw near to it.

Understandably, David had a few things to sort out like what on earth had gone wrong. We'll discuss his findings and his second try next week. For now, let's note two results of David's fear of God that might suggest it had temporarily taken an unhealthy turn. He became ...

1. unwilling (v. 10, "he was not willing")
2. distant (v. 11, "the ark of the Lord remained in the house of Obed-edom ... for three months")

Likewise, when you and I grow unwilling and distant after devastation, even in subtle ways no one else would recognize, our healthy fear of the Lord has momentarily taken an unhealthy turn. God alone knows the number of people in full time ministry – pastors, missionaries, worship leaders, counselors—who have suffered terrible trauma they never worked through with God. They may have remained in their vocations (after all, they often had no other training), but they withdrew their hearts from God and purposed simply to do their jobs.

The problem is, if we're not working in the Spirit, we're defaulting to the flesh. Hence, unresolved personal issues with God have corporate implications and not only for those who work for the church. The misery of having known deep intimacy with God and then withdrawing from it would be almost unbearable. A man or woman after God's own heart couldn't stand it for long.

With the news of God's favor and blessing on his neighbors and a brief passage of time to regroup, David became willing again and most anxious to have the ark—and God's most manifest presence—as close as possible. You know He is life to you and that a sense of His presence is the height of all human experience. If this week's study has dramatically pinpointed your present dilemma, let your Father hold you even if you squirm and your eyes squint from the bright light of His glory. Hear Him whisper in your ear:

"You are My treasure" (Deut. 7:6). "Return to me with all your heart" (Joel 2:12).

VIEWERGUIDE

MOVING ON WITH BRAVE OBEDIENCE

God is not interested in just adjusting our lives. He wants us transformed.
A full-fledged so far transformation requires that

(From session 3)
1. We've got to move past our devastation with God. David was …
   • Angry (v. 8)
   • Afraid (v. 9)

2. We've got to return to _____ obedience. Joy is coming.

    First Chronicles 15:12-15

    Song of Songs 6:12; 2 Samuel 7:20-29

3. Let's have the _____ to see the fulfillment of God's promises to us.

Your God has good things for you—not _____ things for you, good things for you.

DISCUSSION QUESTIONS

1. Did you ever do anything you knew was wrong as a child? Why did you do it? How did you feel about it later? Were you disciplined by your parents?

2. How do you feel as an adult when you realize you have sinned? How do you feel when you know you are walking in close obedience to God?

WEEK FOUR | DAY ONE
Back to the Prescribed Way

"It was because you, the Levites, did not bring it up the first time that the LORD our God broke out in anger against us. We did not inquire of Him about how to do it in the prescribed way" (1 Chron. 15:13, NIV).

Hey, Sweet Thing! I'm so glad you came back. Once people get a clue about what they've gotten themselves into, I never know for sure if I'll ever see them again. I've said many times that my "style," if you can call it that, is so obnoxious that I don't think I'd attend my own classes … but I guess you understand that I have to. You, on the other hand, don't. So I'm grateful that you did. I praise God for having the privilege to serve with Priscilla and Kay on this project. If I drive you crazy, just hang on for a little while and one of them will come to the rescue.

As we start our fourth week of study together, I want to share with you a tad of insight I gleaned from my favorite two-year-old. My darling grandson, Jackson, is learning to make faces that you can tell he's already attached to certain emotions. Smart thing.

To our unending delight, we often catch Jackson practicing these faces when his eye catches a mirror. He pauses suddenly as if he'd hate to the miss the opportunity to stare at himself and then begins the experiment. He smiles really big; then he frowns as hard as he can, drawing his eyebrows down so far that they crowd his plump cheeks. He proceeds with his best mad face and sometimes even flexes his muscles for emphasis.

Jackson's favorite face to practice, however, is the pout. It takes the most effort and often gets the most attention. He rolls his bottom lip out as far as he can, turns down the edges of his mouth and gets a look in his eye like he's about to cry. He then freezes the expression as long as he can. Sometimes I even see him practice it while he's playing. By the time he gets an opportunity to show his displeasure over something his parents or grandparents won't let him do, he's practiced-up. Out pops the lip. I'd laugh out loud if I didn't think it would lead straight into the mad face.

The thought occurred to me a few days ago that full-grown adults can practice the pout so long that it becomes our first natural reaction to anything negative or inconvenient. Don't get me wrong. You and I have been talking about authentic devastations that only God can get us through. Grieving is a thousand country miles from pouting. I want to interject, however, that if we resist the grace of God and do not let Him tend to us and bring us healing over time, we can develop into life-style pouters.

1. Hebrews 12:15 describes what can happen. What does it warn against and why?

What exactly does a pouter want from people? I'll throw an answer on the table since I enjoy a good pout as much as anyone, and I'll use an acronym because I love word games more than emotional games. A pouter wants people to feel sorry for her for being such a Poor Ole Unloved Thing. Do you think it fits?

2. If you can think of a good acronym for POUT, throw yours on the table here:

P_____

O_____

U_____

T_____

Pretty fun, isn't it? Unfortunately, for all the attention a pouter wants, even what she gets will backfire on her because, frankly, nobody likes a pouter. Sometimes we feel so sorry for ourselves that we don't leave room for anyone else to feel sorry for us—even when we could legitimately use some pity.

We don't have to make sure everyone knows how unhappy we are to have our pain acknowledged. Instead, we can take it to God. He cares. He knows. He heals. Just about the time we quit craving the pity of others, He also brings someone along the path to flesh-out a loving touch from His hand.

This week we'll continue to explore answers to the question presented in session 3: How can we cooperate with God for a work that will leave us in awe saying, "Who am I, O Sovereign LORD, and what is my family that you have brought me this far?" We're deriving our answers from the life of David because he initiated the question.

We spent the majority of our third week of study on the first proposal: If we're going to move forward with God to a "this far" kind of place, we've got to move past our devastation with God. Our second answer came from the beginning of session 4: We've got to return to wholehearted obedience. Write the words "wholehearted obedience" in capital letters in the margin.

Let's clear up a matter as quickly in print as we did on video so that no one develops an offense and quits the study. Often our suffering has absolutely no connection to disobedience. Disease and tragedy visit the innocent as well as the guilty.

3. Take a look at Matthew 5:45 and fill in the remainder of this sentence: "He causes his sun to rise on the ...

Our God is unbelievably gracious and long suffering. Even so, we'll make a grievous mistake not to emphasize the role of obedience in moving "this far" with God. Here are a few reasons:

UNTREATED DISAPPOINTMENT LEADS TO DISOBEDIENCE

A formerly obedient child can let disappointment lead her to disobedience. As we discussed in session 4, our devastation may have nothing to with disobedience, but if we don't deal with our disappointment about God's sovereign decisions, we'll default our way into disobedience.

4. Read Psalm 40:12 (NIV) and fill in the following blanks:

"For _____ without number surround me; my _____ have overtaken me, and I cannot see. They are more than the hairs of my head, and my heart fails within me."

Carefully note that the process toward the psalmist's spiritual heart failure began with terrible "troubles" before proceeding into "sins." His troubles may well have come on him like rain on the innocent. But if he resisted God's help and healing, trouble could have led to sin like the tide sweeping over a hermit crab.

Let me give you an example. I was completely innocent of my childhood abuse, but I lost my innocence when I disobeyed God's Word, resisted honesty and divine restoration, and defaulted in anger, hatred, and immorality. Troubles first surrounded me, and then sins overtook me.

5. Have you experienced something that began as troubles but grew into sin? Share it here.

What positive lessons has God taught you through the painful circumstance?

What painful costs has the sin brought into your life?

MOVING FORWARD DEMANDS OBEDIENCE

We'll never take a step forward with God without obedience. That's the simple long and short of it.

6. What did God tell His people in Jeremiah 7:23?

7. According to Jeremiah 7:24, what did they do instead?

8. Which direction did they end up going? _____

David's devastation was directly related to disobedience and therefore vital to our series. That's where we'll pick up now. In our session we looked at 1 Chronicles 15:11-15 briefly, but let's give it another glance to solidify our context. Turn there now.

9. According to verse 13, what was the exact reason God's anger broke out against the Israelites and not just against Uzzah?

In session 4 we talked about the terrible mistake the Israelites made when they did not seek to transport the ark in God's prescribed way. In tomorrow's lesson we'll see the Scriptures dictating the written instructions they should have heeded. Now return to 2 Samuel 6 and let's revisit the consequence.

At times when God almost seems mean-spirited to us, we have the opportunity to discover whether we have based our faith on who God is or on what He does.

Because God's ways are higher than our ways, we cannot always comprehend what He is doing or why He makes certain decisions. When we sift His apparent activity through the standard of who He is, we will invariably and ultimately find relief and healing. Basing our faith on who God is rather than what He appears to be doing is crucial to our spiritual health; therefore, let's practice this approach as we conclude today's lesson.

10. Reread 2 Samuel 6:1-12 but this time with your eye on one goal. List every single thing this text conveys to you about who God is and next to it the portion of Scripture that helped you arrive at your conclusion.

Who God is . . .   How you know . . .

Let's wrap up today's lesson with a bottom line that will bridge us to day 2:

God is not ~~harsh~~. He is *holy.*

Big difference, Darling One. **BIG DIFFERENCE.**

WEEK FOUR | DAY TWO

Fresh Reverence

"Exalt the Lord our God and worship at his holy mountain,
for the Lord our God is holy" (Ps. 99:9, NIV).

1. We concluded yesterday's lesson with an important bottom line. Write it here:

Sometimes I wish I'd lived during eras when God parted waters, rained down manna, spoke through thunder, and led by cloudy pillars. Do you? Needless to say, He still could. After all, He's the same God. In His kingdom agenda, however, it would be redundant because the One to whom the Old Covenant pointed has come. We need not paint our doorposts with the blood of lambs to protect us from the angel of death.

2. Read 1 Corinthians 5:7 and record the reason here.

3. Likewise, we need not retreat to the wilderness and strike a rock to get water. Read 1 Corinthians 10:3-4 and record the reason here.

4. Furthermore, we don't need to climb out of bed and look on the ground for manna from heaven. Read John 6:51 and record the reason here.

5. We don't need priests to transport the ark. Record the reason here (Heb. 6:19-20).

As we continue to reflect on 2 Samuel 6 and the disobedience that resulted in the death of Uzzah, let's try to grasp the glory that was at stake and the lesson that had to be taught. We have difficulty understanding the sacred nature of the ark of the covenant because we have the advantage of living after the incarnation of Christ.

Think with me about the representation of the ark and how we can only compare it to Christ Himself, the Word made flesh to dwell among us. Once man and woman were cast from the intimate presence of God's fellowship in the garden of Eden, God began His ministry of reconciliation, which He ultimately fulfilled through the cross. Through the centuries after our expulsion from the garden no one, not even Abraham had an invitation to come and experience direct fellowship with God. At last God spoke revolutionary words to His servant, Moses.

6. Write Exodus 25:8 here:

What music to their needy ears! In the innermost place in this "sanctuary," God commanded them to build the ark of the covenant according to very specific directions. Then He said, "There, above the cover between the two cherubim that are over the ark of the Testimony, I will meet with you" (Ex. 25:22, NIV). The awesomeness, the holiness, and the majesty of God dwelled right there, between the cherubim on that sacred ark!

Until God was incarnate among men many centuries later in the person of Jesus Christ, the ark was the sacred center of God's glory and presence. To treat the ark inappropriately was to treat God inappropriately, not just because of what it was but who God was. Who God *is*. Now, based on who God is, can we draw any sound conclusions about what He was doing that day? I believe we can draw at least four.

1. GOD WAS SETTING GROUND RULES FOR A NEW REGIME.

God was ushering in a new kingdom with a new king He had chosen to represent His heart. He dealt with the disrespect of man through many judges and the reign of a selfish king. With a new day dawning, God was demanding a new reverence. I believe Uzzah's outward act very likely may have been an indicator of an inward attitude. Remember, God does not look on the outward appearance but on the heart.

I believe this corporate concept can also apply to each individual. Every time God has a new day of sorts dawning in my life, He also demands a new reverence from me. Every time He has a new place to take me, He has something new about His holiness He seems to want to show me. God seems to say, "This revelation involves a responsibility that can only come with reverence."

7. Have you ever experienced something similar? If so, describe it.

2. GOD WANTED HIS CHILDREN TO BE DIFFERENT FROM THE WORLD.

God would not accept attitudes and approaches from His children that were no different from those of the godless. Recall again how the Israelites attempted to transport the ark. We mentioned their decisive error in judgment in our session and in our previous lesson, but now let's take a better look at it. In 1 Samuel 6, we discover that the Philistine army had captured the ark; then after being struck with plagues, they sought to return it. I don't blame them.

8. How did the Philistines transport the ark (1 Sam. 6:7-8)?

Fast forward to 2 Samuel 6. Do you see the broader implications of what Israel had done? They had copied the methods of a heathen people that didn't even call on the name of their God. How careful we must be not to think that God is less holy because others seem to get away with irreverence! I vividly remember the many times my children said to me in response to a scolding, "But _____ does it!" or "_____ says it!"

I said the same thing to my children you who are moms probably say to yours: "Those are not my children. I expect something different from you because of who you are and what you know." We are sometimes tempted to measure our respect for God by the lack of respect surrounding us. The godless, however, are not our standard. God is. Through the pen of David, God told us to "praise him according to his excellent greatness," not according to public opinion (Ps. 150:2, KJV).

3. GOD WANTED HIS KINGDOM ESTABLISHED ON HIS WORD.

The Israelites had made the mistake of transporting the ark by the same method the Philistines used—without consulting God's designated commands for its transportation. At the time David's kingdom was established, David certainly had access to the Books of Moses, the first five books of the Bible. We've talked about what they should have done, but let's now read the instructions for ourselves

9. Read Exodus 25:10-16 and Numbers 4:5,15. What did God's Word prescribe for transporting the ark?

We're learning that God masterfully designed the transportation of His glory to literally rest on the shoulders of His revering priests, not on the backs of beasts. Believers in Christ make up the priesthood today.

10. In what ways can we apply the principle of 1 Peter 2:9 to ourselves?

4. GOD WAS TEACHING THE RELATIONSHIP BETWEEN BLESSING AND REVERENCE.

God revealed the relationship through the effects of the ark on Obed-edom and his household. God desires His presence and His glory to be a blessing, but reverence for Him is the necessary channel. Hard lessons learned well undoubtedly usher in a fresh respect and new freedom. As strange as this statement may seem, the more we learn about God and the more we practice a healthy fear of Him, the more freedom we have to worship Him! We'll see this principle at work in David's life tomorrow.

Thank you for your hard work today! May God write these truths on your heart and transport a fresh revelation to your household on your sweet shoulders.

WEEK FOUR | DAY THREE

To Dance with All Your Might

"David, wearing a linen ephod, danced before the LORD with all his might" (2 Sam. 6:14, NIV).

1. You and I have been talking about cooperating with God so that He can take us enough miles from where we began that with awe and thanksgiving we can respond like this: (See if you can fill in the blanks from memory now!)

"_____, O Sovereign LORD, and _____,
that you have _____" (2 Sam. 7:18)?

2. So far, we've discussed two proposals. Write them both here:

We've got to move past _____.

We've got to return to _____.

In today's lesson we'll see where David had cooperated with God in both these vital actions and the dividend was astronomical. By this time you're ready for some good news in our print work so let's go get it!

3. Please relish a reread of 2 Samuel 6:11-15 and take time to picture it. Describe the portrait of David that this segment paints:

4. List at least four adjectives you believe describe how David felt that day as he danced before the Lord with all his might.

_____   _____

_____   _____

I'm not sure any experience between man and his God is quite like the resurrection of copious praise after a season he thought would nearly kill him. We've talked about the terrible complication of experiencing devastation at a time of expected celebration, but now we have an opportunity to view it in reverse.

We can endure something so horrific that we can convince ourselves life is over for us. We can conclude that all joy is behind us and only pain awaits in the future. But, if we're willing, one day at a time, one layer at a time, God begins to bring healing, restoration, and perhaps best of all, fresh revelation. Little slivers of light turn into late dawns and, finally, noon day suns.

When the love of God calls forth a love for God in a heart of brokenness, it spills forth in a way no happy heart can gush. I can remember the exact moment I realized I was going to survive a season of loss and grave defeat. With the pain still present in my heart but strumming now in clear, acoustical praise, I felt oddly more alive than I'd ever been in my life. The scars on my battered soul no longer appeared to me as random slashes but suddenly transfigured into engravings of unexpected praise and thanksgiving.

God had done and been exactly what He'd said He would. To the secret places of our souls, where doubt hides and mocks, God's ability to restore remains a blessed theory until we experience His sustaining power for ourselves.

I wouldn't trade that intense season with my Redeemer for anything in this world. I lived off of Him and His promises hour by hour. I failed Him but He neither failed me nor left me in my failure. He stood me to my feet and began to form Christ in me (Gal. 4:19) in ways this former pit-dweller would have sworn were impossible. I have a long way to go, but I am so far from where I was that He alone could be the excuse. Bless His holy name!

That very season turned me into a true worshiper more than any pleasant season of my life. Meanwhile, I still lacked answers to most of my questions but I didn't lack the fullness of God in my painful experience.

5. Have you ever experienced anything similar? If so, describe it briefly here:

I wish I could hear your story. My faith would be so encouraged.

6. Glance back at 2 Samuel 6:14. How does it describe David's dance before the Lord?

When was the last time you and I did anything "with all our might"? We're so overworked and hyperactive that we often feel too scattered to do *anything* with *everything* we possess. I want so much to give God my everything. Don't you? I'm never any happier or feel any healthier than when I'm completely caught up—spirit, soul, and body—in praise and adoration of Jesus. To abandon myself completely in worship is the ultimate act of freedom to me.

Worship with abandon is an intimate experience and one we may not often get to express publicly. A comprehensive study of David will reveal to us that he didn't dance (and leap, v. 16!) down the streets of Jerusalem dressed in priestly attire as a daily routine, but that particular day in the nation of Israel nothing was more appropriate or compulsory. The man after God's own heart could not hold himself back, and thankfully, the circumstances made no such demand.

7. **Even though the king was well within the bounds of propriety that special day, read 2 Samuel 6:16-23 and record each way his wife, Michal (pronounced me-KAWL), reacted to the scene.**

8. **How did David react?**

9. **Has anyone ever ridiculed or looked down on you for your abandoned worship to the Lord? If so, without using names, what were the circumstances?**

It's painful, isn't it? And later on, sometimes it's embarrassing. Occasionally I'll see a picture someone took of me during praise and worship at an event (a questionable time for cameras), and I'll feel silly or maybe even insulted. I always want to say, "You can't understand the praise outside the atmosphere. It was publicly appropriate in its God-blessed context!"

10. **The Gospels record several other occasions when lavish worshipers were rebuked or criticized. You'll find an example in John 12:1-8. Read this segment and describe the act of worship.**

11. **Who criticized it and why?**

Everyone who understands enough about God to pour her life lavishly on His altar will be misunderstood by someone who doesn't. The quagmire is that if we're not careful, we'll develop a self-righteous, judgmental attitude toward the person and end up in more sin than our offender.

12. **Let's look carefully now at 2 Samuel 6:16. Where was Michal when she watched David enter Jerusalem? Select one.**

   * At a window   * In the palace   * On the hilltop   * On a chariot

I've studied these verses many times, but a question rises up in me this time that I'm not sure I've considered before: Why was Michal watching from a window instead of taking part in the ceremony? As a woman in her ancient culture, perhaps she couldn't have been part of the official processional, but we know without a doubt that women participated in the celebration.

13. Second Samuel 6:18-19 describe David's blessing on all the people and the gifts he gave "both _____ and _____." (Fill in the blank according to v. 19.)

14. We also know that even the servant girls partook in the grand festivities because Michal accused David of vulgarity in front of them. What was Michal's problem? Offer your thoughts:

15. Some people are threatened by a loved one's lavish affection and devotion to God. Can you think of several reasons why? Offer them here.

To worship God alone is to refuse to worship a person no matter how dear to you he or she may be. To seek God first is to seek even the most cherished person in your life second. To obey God rather than man means that you might end up doing something a man or woman in your life doesn't want you to do: something right and something loving because God does nothing otherwise.

Still, a person in your life may feel threatened over your decision of obedience to God because it clearly isn't all about him or her. Like Judas, they may fear there's nothing in it for them and they may pout, but make no mistake. They are no poor ole unloved thing. God loves them as much as He loves you, and His plan is best for you both.

People who don't understand wholehearted devotion to Christ also don't grasp that He will never ask something of one person that is not also and ultimately best for the other.

His insistence that we let no one rival His place in our lives is as much for others as for us and for His glory. No human being can bear the burden of being worshiped no matter how we crave it.

WEEK FOUR | DAY FOUR

Mourning Turned to Dancing

*"You turned my wailing into dancing; you removed my sackcloth
and clothed me with joy" (Ps. 30:11, NIV).*

Yesterday we studied David dancing "with all his might" down the streets of Jerusalem in unbridled praise to his God. We also touched on the reality that a public place was not the regular locale of his everyday worship. Had David always broken out in a praise dance every time he participated in public worship, he probably would've become little more than an object of distraction and ultimately disdain.

Surely one reason God considered David a man after His own heart was that the depth of his private worship exceeded the height of every public expression. The psalms he penned in the open fields while herding sheep and in the craggy clefts while hiding from Saul are proof. The most moving among them are those addressed to God as "You" and David as "me."

That's where it happens. Without a doubt, the depth and breadth our personal relationships with God are defined in the private places with a population of two. If we restrict ourselves to public places of worship, no matter how genuine the atmosphere, our growth will remain stunted and our praise will become staged. Those of us who love corporate worship must be doubly guarded against the temptation to perform.

1. Offer a few ways our praise can become performance oriented:

Today we're going to take the things we learned yesterday about the heights of praise that can erupt after a season of pain and personalize them through our own psalm. I can't think of a better inspired song of David to set the tone than Psalm 30. Please read Psalm30—aloud if at all possible. As you do, feel the emotion of it.

2. List each way David described the depths to which he'd plunged:

3. Now list each way he described the heights that he presently felt:

4. What title would you give this psalm? _____

5. What was David's point to God in verse 9?

You and I have the joyous privilege of living out our tenure after the completion of Scripture. Though the Old Testament prophets believed in resurrection from the dead, they did not have the panoramic picture we behold from a New Testament perspective. You and I get to rejoice in knowing that when we die, our praises to God have barely begun! We will dance and sing and leap with joy in ways we cannot comprehend in these mortal bodies and upon this injured earth. Not only will we join with every tongue, tribe, and nation to praise God before His throne but we will also join the angels of heaven, themselves a sight too much for mortal eyes to bear.

As David hinted in verse 9, these present bodies will turn to dust and these exact hands that hold our Bibles will never be raised in praise again. However, we will receive new bodies that resemble Christ's with a new unction enabling us to worship without restraint for all eternity.

Free of pride and performance, we will be able to dance with all our might down the streets of the New Jerusalem any time we wish. Even the most contemporary worshiper can join with the hymnist of old who wrote, "When we all get to heaven, what a day of rejoicing that will be! When we all see Jesus, we'll sing and shout the victory!"

We're called to make His praise glorious long before heaven, however. For the remainder of today's lesson we're going to write our own version of Psalm 30 by filling in certain blanks with our own descriptions and testimonials. Reflect once again on yesterday's lesson and, in particular, our discussions on times God restores our joy and praise after a season of devastation.

The Holman Christian Standard version of Psalm 30 appears below with built-in blanks for you to personalize. Please give this exercise some deep thought and make it a sincere confession. This isn't just choir practice. It's the real thing. God is on His throne and His ear is inclined to your voice. He loves you so. Allow the man after God's own heart to help you express what you feel.

Psalm 30:1-12 (HCSB)

1 I will exalt You, LORD, because You have _____ and have
   not allowed _____.

2 LORD my God, I cried to You for help, and You _____ me.

3 LORD, You brought me _____; You
   spared me from _____.

4 Sing to the LORD, you His faithful ones, and praise His holy name.

5 For His _____ lasts only a moment, but His favor, a lifetime. Weeping may spend the night, but there is joy in the morning.

6 When I was secure, I said, _____."

7 Lord, when You showed Your favor, You made me _____ _____; when You _____, I was terrified.

8 LORD, I called to You; I sought favor from my LORD:

9 "What gain is there in _____?

10 LORD, listen and be gracious to me; LORD, be my helper."

11 You turned my _____ into _____; You removed my _____ and clothed me with _____,

12 so that I can sing to You and not be silent. LORD my God, I will praise You forever.

After you've completed the exercise and every blank is filled, go back and read your psalm as sincerest praise to your very personal God.

6. If you're going through a terribly difficult time and you've not yet experienced God turning your mourning to dancing, write a brief prayer below asking Him to grant it to you.

Beloved, let these words sink into the deepest part of your hurting heart: There is no one on earth He loves more than you. He has a hope and a future for you that nothing in your past or present can nullify. When I need the reminder most, no modern-day psalm supplies it more fluidly than "In Christ Alone" by Stuart Townend and Keith Getty. I'll conclude with the portion of the song that I can hardly sing without being overcome with emotion. Receive it as your own.

> No guilt in life, no fear in death,
> This is the power of Christ in me;
> From life's first cry to final breath.
> Jesus commands my destiny.
> No power of hell, no scheme of man,
> Can ever pluck me from His hand;
> Till He returns or calls me home,
> Here in the power of Christ I'll stand.

(© 2001, Kingsway Thank You Music)

WEEK FOUR | DAY FIVE

Hanging Onto the Blessing

"Now be pleased to bless the house of Your servant, that it may continue forever in Your sight; for You, O Sovereign LORD, have spoken" (2 Sam. 7:29, NIV).

Dear Sister, this is my last day to lead the discussion, but with joy I'll walk with you through the remaining two weeks of our journey. Priscilla and I gladly defer to Kay as the wisest and most knowledgeable of women Bible teachers. I've been around her many times and not once have I seen her act or speak inconsistently with the person she appears to be on the platform. You can rest assured that the relationship she seems to have with God in public is passionately sought with God in private. I respect her so much. Don't miss the last two weeks of study.

Today we'll return to the text where we began our time together in session 3. Please read 2 Samuel 7:18-29; in just a moment we'll begin to take it apart in segments and discuss it.

1. **What question have we grappled with through both sessions and both weeks of study? Complete the sentence: How can you and I cooperate with God so that He can …**

2. **In the sessions I offered you three answers based on the life of the man after God's own heart. Recall the first two and complete each sentence:**

   We've got to get past our _____.

   We've got to return to _____.

I offered you the third proposal at the end of our last session together.

3. **Let's have the courage to see the fulfillment of God's promises.**

This point was based on David's marvelous confession in verses 27-29. Glance at them again then please allow me to paraphrase it this way: "So, Lord, if You really want to bless me and really want to do all of these astonishing things for me, I'm going to have the courage to receive it! After all, who am I to stop You? You have spoken! Go ahead and do what You said!"

Oh, to have the courage to receive the promises of God! And, oh, for the bravery to stand to our feet and become persons He can stunningly bless to the glory of His name! Let's see a few ways that receiving blessing requires bravery based on this segment of Scripture.

First fasten your gaze on verse 19. David asked an important question that we touched on in session 3. "Is this Your usual way of dealing with man, O Sovereign LORD?" The answer, particularly this side of Christ's cross, is a resounding "Yes!" God doesn't just redeem on occasion. He is the Redeemer. It's His job! It's what He does because it's who He is. He buys captives back from slavery and restores the surrendered fortunes of their son-ship.

The times I've been in deepest need of forgiveness have been the very times I felt most shamed and reluctant to come to Christ to receive it. That's the destructive power of self-condemnation. It lies and keeps us from the cross. I hated so badly to have to ask Him to help me out of another mess. Although God has no intention of cooperating with us while we keep returning to sin (hence, the whole concept of chastisement), He is never reluctant to forgive the repentant.

4. What does Micah 7:18-19 tell you about God?

Second, God's "usual way" is not only to redeem the captive and to forgive the repentant. His usual way of dealing with man is to bless.

5. What do the following New Testament Scriptures tell you about God's blessings?

    John 1:14,16

    Ephesians 1:3

Second Samuel 7:20-21 records one of the most astonishing parts of God's usual way of blessing: "For you know your servant, O Sovereign LORD. For the sake of your word and according to your will you have done this great thing." Let this sink into your heart and soul: God knows us thoroughly and reads us constantly (Ps. 139:1-4). He knows you, Beloved. And He chose you. He knows me too. Chose me too. No wonder the psalmist suddenly exclaimed, "How great You are, O Sovereign LORD! There is no one like You!"

Third, Dear One, we have to be courageous enough to acknowledge with our entire body, soul, and spirit that there's utterly no one like God.

6. If you've come to that unshakable conclusion in your own life, what experience did God use most to teach it to you?

Praise God for it, Beloved, even if it was horrifically painful. Some people live a lifetime without ever allowing themselves to admit that the Lord God of heaven and earth has no equal.

Take a good look at verse 23. What a magnificent truth it tells us! Because there is no one like God, no group of people are like His people. That promise includes us, the grafted branches (Rom. 11:17) and the spiritual seed of Abraham (Gal. 3:29). The concept of our uniqueness as a people because of the uniqueness of our God is underscored many times in Scripture. Deuteronomy 33:29 is one of my favorites and I pray it often for my family.

"Who is like you, a people saved by the Lord? He is the shield that protects you, the sword you boast in. Your enemies will cringe before you, and you will tread on their backs" (Deut. 33:29 HCSB).

Hallelujah! God wants us to be brave and act like a people unlike any other on earth.

"In all these things we are more than conquerors through him who loved us" (Rom. 8:37).

I don't know about you, but I may have to stand up and do a praise dance. Anyway, nobody's watching but God. Second Samuel 7:25-26 makes clear that one way God has chosen to display the greatness of His name is to do as He has promised regarding His people. Oh, Beloved, God desires to do such extraordinary things for and through us if we accept that everything is for His glory. Romans 11:36 says it perfectly: "For from Him and through Him and to Him are all things. To Him be the glory forever. Amen" (HCSB).

7. **Since I'm a woman, I love nothing better than seeing a woman in Scripture receive a divine promise. I'm crazy about the way Mary received the promise of God concerning the Messiah in Luke 1:38. Take it look at it for yourself. What did she say?**

8. **Not coincidentally, Mary's relative, Elizabeth, had a coinciding blessing for her in Luke 1:45. What was it?**

Take Mary's words and Elizabeth's blessing personally. No, God has not promised us the same things He promised them, but make no mistake. God has made us plenty of promises and He is faithful to His Word. As we conclude our portion of this journey, I want you to gather your courage as David did and offer God a prayer. Thank Him for all He's spoken over your life, even what you do not yet know, because you can trust His goodness. Ask Him to empower you to cooperate with Him until you, in awe, can say, "Who am I, O Sovereign LORD, and who is my family that You have brought me this far?" Ask Him not to lift His hand until He has made His name great before your entire family. Then, have the courage to ask for your entire family line up to the return of Christ to experience an astonishing "so far" work of God.

Oh, Dear One, so often we have not because we ask not (Jas. 4:2). God is huge. Muster the courage to ask huge things of Him. As long as you keep His glory the point and priority of every petition, ask to your heart's content! He will bless your pure heart and your devoted life even in those times when He knows better than to bless you with your momentary desire. You are His treasure. A woman He's making after His own heart. Thank you so, so much for granting me the unspeakable privilege of serving you. In closing, please allow me to pray the words of David in 2 Samuel 7:28-29 over your deeply significant life. As I do, Girlfriend, receive them!

"O Sovereign LORD, you are God! Your words are trustworthy, and you have promised good things to your servant. Now be pleased to bless the house of your servant, that it may continue forever in your sight; for you, O Sovereign LORD, have spoken, and with your blessing the house of your servant will be blessed forever." In the delivering name of Jesus—the Son of David, the Son of man, the beloved and only Son of God—I ask these things for Your great glory. Amen.

KAYARTHUR

REDEEMED

VIEWERGUIDE

SIN IS DEADLY

Scriptures That Tell Us What Sin Is

1. **James 4:17** Sin is to know the _____ _____ and not do it.

2. **First John 3:4** Sin is _____. It means that you are not going to keep the law of God.

3. **First John 5:17** All _____ is sin. To not do what is right in the eyes of God is sin.

4. **Romans 14:23** Whatever is not of _____ is sin.

Five Things About Sin
2 Samuel 11–12; 1 Chronicles 11:41

1. Sin will take you _____ than you ever intended to go.

2. When you sin, you are _____ God (2 Sam. 12:9).

3. Sin is _____ (2 Sam. 12:9).

4. The temptation to sin is _____ _____ than you can bear (1 Cor. 10:13).

5. Sin costs you more than you _____ to pay (Num. 32:23).

GROUP DISCUSSION QUESTIONS

1. What are some ways the word *redeemed* is used in the secular world? How do those images connect to the Christian meaning of the word?

2. What did God's grace mean to you at the time of your salvation? What does it mean to you today?

WEEK FIVE | DAY ONE

Costly Crossroads

"In the spring, at the time when kings go off to war, David sent Joab out with the king's men and the whole Israelite army" (2 Sam. 11:1 NIV).

Beware of triumph, the confidence of success, its glory and the entitlements thought to go with it. The road to glory is more than a spectacular pinnacle. Yes, beloved, triumph can lead to the mountaintop where the view is so breathtaking that you spread your arms triumphantly to dance with the wind. However, seldom does one build a home and live on the heights forever.

As you've seen in your studies with Priscilla and Beth, David has come to the pinnacle of power. Now David is:

- King over all Israel
- Magnet of valiant mighty men—all loyal volunteers who had made it their business to turn all the kingdom to the man they loved
- Defeater of the Philistines and triumphant over the opposition

Although David was denied the privilege of building a house for God, the Lord blessed him with the covenant promise of a house that would endure forever. Indeed, this king was:

- Father to 18 sons and a daughter by the name of Tamar
- Head of the armies of Israel, exercising the luxury of staying home

Success, triumph, achievements—they all put us at crossroads. We've achieved a major goal. What is next? Where will we go now? What will we do next?

What happened to King David after all this? I want you to find out for yourself, beloved, because nothing is more effective than discovering truth for yourself and then digging deeper into it, mining and adorning yourself with its treasures. You may be about to reread a familiar story or to read it for the first time. While we are not going to camp on it, we do need to see it so we can put the rest of David's life in context. In doing so, we will see what we are to do when we come to our own crossroads in life.

CROSSROADS ARE DECISIONS

Since we might have various understandings of what crossroads are, let me give you my definition for the purpose of this study. I am using *crossroads* to indicate the times when we have to make a choice as to the direction we will take—that is all. Every decision leads us somewhere. Having just taught some new friends who captured my heart—friends who happen to live in two prisons in Arkansas—*crossroads* takes on a greater significance as I think of the gravity of our decisions. Like my new friends, many of us don't stop to think about the consequences of our choices and where they will take us.

I know I must live more purposefully. I love life. I love new things. I think I can do more than I can do, and I don't want to miss out on anything. I love the mission, the call, the challenge— and I don't want to miss the party, even (and especially) at my age!

GOD'S WORD IS TRUTH

Now let's observe David at the crossroads he faced. I want us to observe 2 Samuel 11:1-17 and see what the text tells us about three people: David, Bathsheba, and Uriah. When you study the Bible inductively—in other words, when you go straight to the Word of God yourself to discover what it says, what it means, and how you are to line up your thinking and behavior with truth— you begin observing the things that are the easiest to see—most often, people.

Now, beloved, read through the text and color-code every reference to each of these people—the major players in this portion of the chapter. (Color-coding helps you highlight information you discover and to see similarities throughout Scripture.) If you don't know what colors to use, you may want to color references to David in purple (a royal color); to Bathsheba, in red, because in David's eyes she was "hot"; and to Uriah, in orange. If you don't have colored pencils, then use symbols: a square for David, a circle for Bathsheba, and an underline for Uriah's name.

2 Samuel 11:1-17, NASB

1 *Then it happened in the spring, at the time when kings go out to battle, that David sent Joab and his servants with him and all Israel, and they destroyed the sons of Ammon and besieged Rabbah. But David stayed at Jerusalem.*

2 *Now when evening came David arose from his bed and walked around on the roof of the king's house, and from the roof he saw a woman bathing; and the woman was very beautiful in appearance.*

3 *So David sent and inquired about the woman. And one said, "Is this not Bathsheba, the daughter of Eliam, the wife of Uriah the Hittite?"*

4 *David sent messengers and took her, and when she came to him, he lay with her; and when she had purified herself from her uncleanness, she returned to her house.*

5 *The woman conceived; and she sent and told David, and said, "I am pregnant."*

6 *Then David sent to Joab, saying, "Send me Uriah the Hittite." So Joab sent Uriah to David.*

7 *When Uriah came to him, David asked concerning the welfare of Joab and the people and the state of the war.*

8 *Then David said to Uriah, "Go down to your house, and wash your feet." And Uriah went out of the king's house, and a present from the king was sent out after him.*

9 *But Uriah slept at the door of the king's house with all the servants of his lord, and did not go down to his house.*

10 *Now when they told David, saying, "Uriah did not go down to his house," David said to Uriah, "Have you not come from a journey? Why did you not go down to your house?"*

11 *Uriah said to David, "The ark and Israel and Judah are staying in temporary shelters, and my lord Joab and the servants of my lord are camping in the open field. Shall I then go to my house to eat and to drink and to lie with my wife? By your life and the life of your soul, I will not do this thing."*

12 *Then David said to Uriah, "Stay here today also, and tomorrow I will let you go." So Uriah remained in Jerusalem that day and the next.*

13 *Now David called him, and he ate and drank before him, and he made him drunk; and in the evening he went out to lie on his bed with his lord's servants, but he did not go down to his house.*

14 *Now in the morning David wrote a letter to Joab and sent it by the hand of Uriah.*

15 *He had written in the letter, saying, "Place Uriah in the front line of the fiercest battle and withdraw from him, so that he may be struck down and die."*

16 *So it was as Joab kept watch on the city, that he put Uriah at the place where he knew there were valiant men.*

17 *The men of the city went out and fought against Joab, and some of the people among David's servants fell; and Uriah the Hittite also died.*

1. Once you mark a word, then you need to see what you learn from marking the text. Therefore, list what you learned from marking **David, Bathsheba**, and **Uriah**.

David	Bathsheba	Uriah

2. Think about what you learned about David. Did you see him at any crossroads? If so, put an X at any verse that shows him at a point of decision. Then consider the choices David made, why he made them, and whether he could have taken any other path.

Finally, dear child of God, as you go about your day, think about the decisions you are making and their consequences. They may be as simple as whether you should say something or as life changing as whether you stay in a relationship.

3. Think about the ramifications of your decisions. First, are you going against any precept in God's Word? Second, what will be the outcome of your choice? What will it say about your relationship to God? about you as a person?

WEEK FIVE | DAY TWO
❧ Narrow Paths and Broad Roads ❧

"So David sent and inquired about the woman. And one said, 'Is this not Bathsheba, the daughter of Eliam, the wife of Uriah the Hittite?'" (2 Sam. 11:3).

David had made a decision. He wouldn't do what kings were supposed to do at that time of year: go to battle (v. 1). General Joab could go; David was going to stay home. Hadn't he earned the right? David was at a crossroad.

Don't you have a tendency to think that because you have triumphed, achieved victory, won the battle, and accomplished your goal, you can relax? You've done your part. You have succeeded. Don't you deserve a break? Haven't you earned it? A cookie. A reward. A vacation. Watch it; you're at a crossroad. Decisions have consequences.

Right now I'm working on my waistline. Many of my belts no longer fit. Why? Because I let my guard down and started to reward myself for my hard work. I sure enjoyed the candy, the popcorn, the ice cream, the butter, the fat; and the reward didn't show up on the scale the next day. So I got away with it? No! It took a while to show up on my waistline, but show up it did! I sowed to the flesh and reaped more flesh!

But back to David. The view was great from the king's roof. Too good. Tempting. Why on earth didn't David go down into his house and satisfy his awakened desires with one of his wives? Why inquire about something you shouldn't have? Yet, inquire he did. And God in His grace put a red light on David's path. You saw it yesterday, didn't you, in verse 3—one of the places where you marked the references to Bathsheba! You also marked it as a crossroad.

1. What did you learn about Bathsheba in 2 Samuel 11:3?

These details sound rather unnecessary to the story, a little ho-hum, don't they? I am with you. On the surface they do, until we remember God doesn't waste words. Psalm 12:6 tells us every word of God is pure; it came from God's mouth (Deut. 8:3) and serves a purpose. God wants us to know, just as He wanted David to know, that "the woman" David inquired about was the daughter of Eliam, the wife of Uriah, the Hittite.

2. Does that mean anything to David? Look at 2 Samuel 23:34 to find out. Who was Eliam, Bathsheba's father?

3. Now read 2 Samuel 15:12. Who was Ahithophel?

4. Who was Uriah—just a leftover Hittite? Read 1 Chronicles 11:26,41and write your answer. (Verse 26 categorizes the list in which you find Uriah's name, so note "what" Uriah was!)

David was at another crossroad, wasn't he? He should have fled from the situation (2 Tim. 2:22).

5. Now look up these verses. What was Job's personal commitment and the apostle Paul's personal advice?

JOB 31:1,9-12

2 TIMOTHY 2:22

The woman was the granddaughter of his advisor, the wife of one of David's valiant men! Those relationships should have stopped David in his tracks. But did they? Where did David go from his pinnacle of success? Up? Down? Across?

You know the story; you've just read it. However, if you hadn't read it, you've probably heard it. Hollywood loves the story! The world absolutely loves it when God's children blow it. It makes them look better, takes away their guilt, and gives them an excuse.

So where did David head? Did he know what he was doing? Could he help himself? Was he exempt? Could David the king break God's commandments and get away with it? Surely God would protect him, cover him. After all, God had made a covenant with him. Besides, God must have wanted to protect His name and reputation.

6. Now go back to 2 Samuel 11:5. What happened? How did it happen?

7. Now look up the following verses and write down the insights you gain that go with what you just read in 2 Samuel.

GENESIS 29:31

1 SAMUEL 1:5-6

1 SAMUEL 2:6

PSALM 139:15

Was this another crossroad? Of course it was! When we sin, what are we to do? And what will God do? See what you learn from these verses. Remember, these are God's words and He watches over His Word to perform it. God stands by His Word.

PROVERBS 28:13

1 JOHN 1:9

8. What path did David take at this crossroad? Confess or cover? How? Why?

9. What happened next? Any other crossroads where something happened that should have gotten David's attention?

THE CROSSROAD OF NARROW PATHS AND BROAD ROADS

Surely noble David should have been convicted by Uriah's refusal to go home and enjoy the intimacy of his beautiful wife. Surely David winced at Uriah's self-discipline that proved this mighty man of the army more noble than himself (2 Sam. 11:11).

If you ever entertained the lust of infidelity, either mentally or physically, you knew deep in your heart it was wrong. What you did with the conviction put you at a crossroad of two paths: a narrow way of obedience or a broad, crowded road traveled by multitudes but unaccompanied by the blessing of a righteous, holy God.

10. What should David have done next (after 2 Sam.11:11)?

11. What did he do at this crossroad?

12. When that path turned into a dead-end, what came next?

DEAD-END CHOICES

If you listed what you learned from marking the references to Uriah yesterday, you know that he died Let's read the rest of the story. As you do, put a black tombstone like this 🪦 over every reference to death and dying. Color-code or mark mourning by drawing tears like this 💧 . And color-code or mark as you did before the references to *David*, *Bathsheba*, and *Uriah*.

2 Samuel 11:18-27, NASB

18 *Then Joab sent and reported to David all the events of the war.*

19 *He charged the messenger, saying, "When you have finished telling all the events of the war to the king,*

20 *and if it happens that the king's wrath rises and he says to you, 'Why did you go so near to the city to fight? Did you not know that they would shoot from the wall?*

21 *'Who struck down Abimelech the son of Jerubbesheth? Did not a woman throw an upper millstone on him from the wall so that he died at Thebez? Why did you go so near the wall?'—then you shall say, 'Your servant Uriah the Hittite is dead also.' "*

22 *So the messenger departed and came and reported to David all that Joab had sent him to tell.*

23 *The messenger said to David, "The men prevailed against us and came out against us in the field, but we pressed them as far as the entrance of the gate.*

24 *"Moreover, the archers shot at your servants from the wall; so some of the king's servants are dead, and your servant Uriah the Hittite is also dead."*

25 *Then David said to the messenger, "Thus you shall say to Joab, 'Do not let this thing displease you, for the sword devours one as well as another; make your battle against the city stronger and overthrow it'; and so encourage him.' "*

26 *Now when the wife of Uriah heard that Uriah her husband was dead, she mourned for her husband.*

27 *When the time of mourning was over, David sent and brought her to his house and she became his wife; then she bore him a son. But the thing that David had done was evil in the sight of the LORD.*

13. Think about what you just read, beloved. Was Joab taken in by David? Explain your answer.

14. How does David's response to Joab in verse 25 make you feel?

15. What did God think about all this?

16. If you were to stop reading at this point, what might you think happened to David? Does that thinking line up with what you know about God? How about the truth about God? Do you know what the Bible teaches about God?

17. Was David special? Could he, as king, get away with his actions? Why or why not?

18. What do you learn from the last part of Numbers 32:23?

19. Give an example for how Numbers 32:23 applies to you and others today.

WILL GOD WASH HIS HOLY HANDS OF US?

It's sad to learn these difficult things, isn't it, about a man who was described as a man after God's own heart? Surely God had washed His holy hands of David. There would never be another time of dancing with the wind in the triumph of joy.

Or at least that is what you might think if you don't know God very well. Know this, beloved: If you are not dead, no matter what you have done, God is not finished with you.

WEEK FIVE | DAY THREE

Unrepentant Sinner and God's Storyteller

"For whom the Lord loves, He disciplines" (Heb. 12:6).

Nathan was God's man. Nathan feared God more than the king. Thank God for Nathans—those who are strong and courageous, willing to do as God says. Watch how Nathan brought an unrepentant king face-to-face with his sin and nailed him through a story.

FACE-TO-FACE WITH SIN

Read 2 Samuel 12:1-7, and you'll get the picture for yourself—which it's always good to do. Know what the Bible says. Discover truth for yourself and go deep into it. These are words of life.

1. As you read the text printed out below, color-code the references to David as before, follow the points of Nathan's story carefully, and then watch for David's response.

2 Samuel 12:1-7, NASB

1 *Then the* LORD *sent Nathan to David. And he came to him and said,*
   "There were two men in one city, the one rich and the other poor.
2 *"The rich man had a great many flocks and herds.*
3 *"But the poor man had nothing except one little ewe lamb*
   Which he bought and nourished;
   And it grew up together with him and his children.
   It would eat of his bread and drink of his cup and lie in his bosom,
   And was like a daughter to him.
4 *"Now a traveler came to the rich man,*
   And he was unwilling to take from his own flock or his own herd,
   To prepare for the wayfarer who had come to him;
   Rather he took the poor man's ewe lamb and prepared it for the man who had come to him."
5 *Then David's anger burned greatly against the man, and he said to Nathan, "As the* LORD
   lives, surely the man who has done this deserves to die.
6 *"He must make restitution for the lamb fourfold, because he did this thing and had no*
   compassion."
7 *Nathan then said to David, "You are the man!*

2. What was the point of Nathan's telling David this story? What did God want David to see?

3. Why?

Isn't it amazing how we can become so indignant over someone else's sin and miss our own? Or have you noticed that many times when people sin and don't deal with it but instead cover it up, they are quick to anger and to attack others?

Rapidly Heading Down the Mountain

We stopped in the middle of verse 7. Let's go back to the conversation between Nathan and a king who is on a slippery road, headed down the mountain! God isn't finished yet.

4. As you continue reading 2 Samuel 12, mark every reference to:
   • *David* as you have before
   • *God* with a triangle or color all references to Him in yellow
   • *Sin* by coloring it brown

2 Samuel 12:7-15, NASB

7 Nathan then said to David, "You are the man! Thus says the LORD God of Israel, "It is I who anointed you king over Israel and it is I who delivered you from the hand of Saul.

8 "I also gave you your master's house and your master's wives into your care, and I gave you the house of Israel and Judah; and if that had been too little, I would have added to you many more things like these!

9 "Why have you despised the word of the LORD by doing evil in His sight? You have struck down Uriah the Hittite with the sword, have taken his wife to be your wife, and have killed him with the sword of the sons of Ammon.

10 "Now therefore, the sword shall never depart from your house, because you have despised Me and have taken the wife of Uriah the Hittite to be your wife.'

11 "Thus says the LORD, "Behold, I will raise up evil against you from your own household; I will even take your wives before your eyes and give them to your companion, and he will lie with your wives in broad daylight.

12 "Indeed you did it secretly, but I will do this thing before all Israel, and under the sun.'"

13 Then David said to Nathan, "I have sinned against the LORD." And Nathan said to David, "The LORD also has taken away your sin; you shall not die.

14 "However, because by this deed you have given occasion to the enemies of the LORD to blaspheme, the child also that is born to you shall surely die."

15 So Nathan went to his house.

Now, what do you learn from marking the references to the Lord and David? List your insights.

THE LORD	KING DAVID

5. Stop and think about the consequences of David's sin. What was going to happen because of it? Reread verses 10-14 and list what you see in the text, nothing but what is the text. Number the consequences and then compare this list with verse 6, which you marked earlier.

It's one thing to take the whipping yourself and quite another to watch those you love suffer because of your wrong choices at the crossroad.

2 Samuel 12:15-18, NASB

> 15 Then the LORD struck the child that Uriah's widow bore to David, so that he was very sick.
> 16 David therefore inquired of God for the child; and David fasted and went and lay all night on the ground.
> 17 The elders of his household stood beside him in order to raise him up from the ground, but he was unwilling and would not eat food with them.
> 18 Then it happened on the seventh day that the child died.

Read these verses again. I always mark references to *death* and *dying* with a tombstone. "And when lust has conceived, it gives birth to sin; and when sin is accomplished, it brings forth death (Jas. 1:15, NASB). We often forget that the wages of sin is death.

Sin will take you further than you ever wanted to go. It will cost you more than you ever expected to pay. Think about it, beloved. God records all this in His Word for a reason. He wants us to learn from others and remember these things when we come to a crossroad ourselves.

God never changes. He is the same yesterday, today, and forever. It's written in the Law, "be sure your sin will find you out" (Num. 32:23). A holy and just God cannot let sin go unpunished.

WEEK FIVE | DAY FOUR

 God's Unchanging Character

"The child also that is born to you shall surely die" (2 Sam. 12:14, NASB).

God told David that his son would die, but it didn't stop David from fasting and seeking God for his recovery. Did David not believe what God said? I don't know. God doesn't tell us. But David's actions tell us much about his understanding of God. Remember, David was the psalmist. David knew that while God is holy and just, He is also full of loving-kindness, compassion, and mercy. Don't miss this insight because I believe it was David's knowledge of God that sustained him as he harvested his sin and as he was chastened by His God—and rightly so.

David's fasting and sackcloth demonstrated his understanding of the grace of God, as does Psalm 51. Have you ever pondered its truths in the context of David's response to his sin?

DAVID'S RESPONSE

Before one reads the first words of the psalm, we are told the when of its writing, which makes it all the more prized, especially if you have come face-to-face with your sin: "A psalm of David, when Nathan the prophet came to him, after he had gone in to Bathsheba." The entire psalm is printed here because later I want us to come back and go deeper into its precepts. But first simply read it as if you were the person just confronted with your transgressions against a God who had graciously taken you to the heights of success and power.

Psalm 51, NASB

1 *Be gracious to me, O God, according to Your lovingkindness; according to the greatness of Your compassion blot out my transgressions.*

2 *Wash me thoroughly from my iniquity And cleanse me from my sin.*

3 *For I know my transgressions, and my sin is ever before me.*

4 *Against You, You only, I have sinned And done what is evil in Your sight, So that You are justified when You speak And blameless when You judge.*

5 *Behold, I was brought forth in iniquity, And in sin my mother conceived me.*

6 *Behold, You desire truth in the innermost being, And in the hidden part You will make me know wisdom.*

7 *Purify me with hyssop, and I shall be clean; Wash me, and I shall be whiter than snow.*

8 *Make me to hear joy and gladness, Let the bones which You have broken rejoice.*

9 *Hide Your face from my sins And blot out all my iniquities.*

10 *Create in me a clean heart, O God, And renew a steadfast spirit within me.*

11 *Do not cast me away from Your presence And do not take Your Holy Spirit from me.*

12 *Restore to me the joy of Your salvation And sustain me with a willing spirit.*

13 *Then I will teach transgressors Your ways, and sinners will be converted to You.*

14 *Deliver me from bloodguiltiness, O God, the God of my salvation; Then my tongue will
joyfully sing of Your righteousness.*

15 *O LORD, open my lips, That my mouth may declare Your praise.*

16 *For You do not delight in sacrifice, otherwise I would give it; You are not pleased with burnt
offering.*

17 *The sacrifices of God are a broken spirit; A broken and a contrite heart, O God, You will not
despise.*

18 *By Your favor do good to Zion; Build the walls of Jerusalem.*

19 *Then You will delight in righteous sacrifices, In burnt offering and whole burnt offering; then
young bulls will be offered on Your altar.*

LIFE IN HIM

Now read the psalm again, this time focusing on what David knew about God. This is important, beloved, for it is the knowledge of God that keeps us, guarding us from total despair when we have failed, sinned, self-destructed, and yet still live.

Remember, God told David he would not die. He deserved to die. Under the law adultery and murder both warranted death. Yet David lived. How happy I am that he did, for I need to know the lessons we will see as we bring this week to an end and then finish our study next week.

1. As you read Psalm 51 again, mark *God* as you have previously in our study. Don't miss the pronouns. When you finish, list what you observed about God.

Now stop and think: Does God's character change when we sin against Him? The sins of others that are "against us" can turn us inside out. Consequently, we unravel, burst at the seams, and don't behave as we should. But that does not happen to God, and this is what you and I need to remember: God is always approachable. The veil has been torn in two! By one offering we have been sanctified forever (Heb. 10:10,14).

I am never afraid of telling God I've sinned because I know He already knows. There is no need to hide as Adam and Eve did. God had seen their nakedness; it just hadn't occurred to them. They hadn't seen through opened eyes once they knew good and evil.

I know God sees my nakedness. I know there is no hiding from Him. So why try? How foolish to think you can hide from omnipresence.

Bring today to a close by rehearsing what you've learned about God or been reminded of again. Worship Him. Bow before Him and thank Him for being God. How blessed you and I are, beloved, just to be able to do a study like this, to hear and read and study these truths. These are words of life.

WEEK FIVE | DAY FIVE
Grace to Go Deeper Still

"Against You, You only, I have sinned And done what is evil in Your sight, So that You are justified when You speak And blameless when You judge" (Ps. 51:4, NASB).

We must return to Psalm 51 for there is yet more to glean than we have time to allow. How my heart aches for people who do not know God in the depths of truth. How it aches for the vast numbers of women today who don't make the time or effort to discover truth for themselves, go deeper and then disciple others. They are missing life as God intends it and gorging themselves on the husks of the world.

1. Reread Psalm 51 and mark all the references to David and to sin (*iniquity, transgression*). When you finish, summarize what you learned from marking the references to *sin*.

2. Read the psalm again and mark the references to *heart*. How about marking them with a red heart!

   What did you learn?

3. Now what did David want God to do? What did David ask of God? List your insights.

4. How could David——the adulterer, the murderer—ask this of God?

A HEART THAT IS CRUSHED

I'm sure you know what a broken heart is, but do you know what a contrite one is? Contrite means physically and emotionally crushed because of an enemy or because of sin. God does not despise a heart like that. The word for despise in the Hebrew is *bazah* and it means to disesteem, to accord little worth to something, to undervalue, to show contempt.

Think about it. You might despise someone who has blown it with you and has come to ask forgiveness, but God doesn't. And, sweet one, He's not going to start with you. Don't ever make the awful mistake of projecting human feelings and responses onto God. When we do, we get a false God, a false Christ, a false Spirit and we become distorted in our thinking.

5. What most shapes your thinking about God? List some of them.

Human ideas about God	Ideas about God taken from Scripture

6. According to Psalm 51, is life finished after you sin or is there grace to take you deeper still?

What does that answer mean to you in the practical issues of your life?

7. What did David expect, and what did God expect to do?

8. Does this mean David was going to get out of the fourfold judgment of his sin? Since David had a broken and contrite spirit, surely God would let him off the proverbial hook. What do you think and why?

GRACE AFTER THE WRONG TURN

What have you learned this week? How has God personally spoken to your heart and mind? Have you been at a crossroad? Do you now know what path to take?

9. Write down what you have learned; it will be good to someday come back and read what you wrote—or share it with another.

Finally, let's go back to 2 Samuel 12 and see what happened after David and Bathsheba's son died. It will be good information for next week.

2 Samuel 12:24-25, NASB

24 *Then David comforted his wife Bathsheba, and went in to her and lay with her; and she gave birth to a son, and he named him Solomon. Now the LORD loved him*

25 *and sent word through Nathan the prophet, and he named him Jedidiah for the LORD's sake.*

Now, is that grace or not! By the way, Jedidiah means "beloved of the Lord." God gave David and Bathsheba a son, Solomon, beloved of Him.

VIEWERGUIDE

GOD IS GRACIOUS

1. Sin will take you _____ than you ever expected to go; it will keep you _____ than you ever intended to stay, and it will cost you _____ than you ever expected to pay.

Psalm 51

2. What is grace?

3. Grace is _____.

   Charis (Greek): free, unearned, in contrast to something you would earn or something you would work for.

4. Grace is _____ because God is gracious.

5. Grace is _____ (2 Cor. 12:7-10).

6. Grace is _____ (Eph. 1:3).

GROUP DISCUSSION QUESTIONS

1. How has God protected you or stopped you from going too far on a dangerous path? What new insights did you glean about God's grace?

2. How has His power and favor been evident after a wrong turn?

WEEK SIX | DAY ONE

SIN AND CONSEQUENCES

Life is neither easy nor ideal. Rarely is it the dream fulfilled, and it's good to realize that early on. Life is like the first time you get behind the wheel of a car: You're so eager to drive that you barely touch the accelerator and the car either refuses to move or you hit the accelerator too hard and give yourself a scare. You're struggling to navigate all sorts of twists, bends, crossroads, and forks in the road when you're going too fast.

The question is, How are we going to navigate our crossroads? And how are we going to handle what could have been if only … ? Remember what God said to David: "And if that would have been too little, I would have added to you many more things" (2 Sam. 12:8).

How do we handle life when we are worn to the bone or think our hearts are going to rupture because of rejection and pain? when our family is falling apart? How do we go on in the joy of our salvation? How do we teach transgressors His way when we've blown it so badly ourselves? How do we joyfully sing in down times?

Since David spoke of these things in Psalm 51 and experienced these things after "the pinnacle," let's see what we can learn from him. Long after David is dead and buried—but not forgotten— the Book of Acts reminds us again that David was a man after God's own heart. David fulfilled God's purpose in his generation despite his sin.

What lessons can we learn so that we go deeper still with God rather than self-destruct because of failure? Romans 15:4 tells us the things written beforehand (in the Old Testament) are for our instruction that we might have encouragement and hope.

We've seen the first of the fourfold consequences of David's sin; the child born out of David's lust has died. Now comes the family … those closest and usually dearest to us. Remember God's words from earlier days in our study?

> "'Now, therefore, the sword shall never depart from your house, because you have despised Me and have taken the wife of Uriah the Hittite to be your wife?' Thus says the Lord, 'Behold I will raise up evil against you from your own household; I will even take your wives before your eyes and give them to your companion, and he will lie with your wives in broad daylight'" (2 Sam. 12:10-11).

1. Read 2 Samuel 13 in your Bible. As you do, may I suggest you mark your Bible—even if just a little bit. You'll find doing so will help you recall what is happening in the chapter.
   * Mark *heart* and *love*. How about using a red heart for both?
   * Mark *hate* with a black heart.
   * Put a black tombstone over any reference to **death** or **dying**.

When you finish, come back and we'll summarize what you learned from this chapter.

2. Who are the main characters in this chapter? List them along with a brief description of who they are.

3. Now what happened in this chapter? Summarize the events.

4. Do you see anything that might reflect God's judgment when He said, "The sword shall never depart from your house"(2 Sam. 12:10)? We'll share more together tomorrow, beloved.

WEEK SIX | DAY TWO
Persevering Through Discipline

It isn't easy to watch your family fall apart. Maybe you too, like David, have mourned over a son or a daughter. It was just the beginning of David's sorrows. As you read on in 2 Samuel you find David and Absalom's relationship deteriorating until Absalom was in open warfare with his father, seeking his kingdom and his life.

I wonder if there is anything more painful or heart-wrenching than to have the child of your womb turn against you. It is one thing to watch your child self-destruct; but another to have him or her try to destroy you, take away your power or authority, or dishonor you by breaking one of God's commandments and openly shaming and disdaining you before others! Absalom slept with his father's wives by erecting a tent on the housetop (the housetop from which David watched Bathsheba!) and blatantly going into them in the sight of all Israel.

When David heard of it, did he hear the echo of God's words, "I will even take your wives before your eyes and give them to your companion, and he will lie with your wives in broad daylight. Indeed you did it secretly, but I will do this thing before all Israel and under the sun" (2 Sam. 12:11-12)?

If you were to continue in 2 Samuel, you would read of David covering his face, weeping, and crying in utter agony, "O my son, Absalom, O Absalom, my son, my son!"

The son died. The father lived. David wished it had been the opposite, but in God's sovereignty, it wasn't. Joab pierced Absalom as he hung from a tree, caught by his glorious head of hair. David lived on as king, returning to Jerusalem. Even though life did not get easier, David pressed on. Persevering without becoming bitter, the king humbled himself under God's mighty hand and took God's discipline as a true son of God.

How important it is that we follow David's example! David did not fail to appropriate the all-sufficient grace of God. This takes me to Hebrews 12, which is often referred to as the chastening chapter, the chapter that tells us the benefits of the Lord's discipline on our lives. You will find a portion of it printed here because I want to make sure you see these precepts of life for yourself.

1. As you read Hebrews 12:5-15, color-code or mark the following words:
   discipline in any form, including synonyms such as **endure, healed, grace**.
   When you come to an instruction, underline it.

Hebrews 12:5-15, NASB

5 and you have forgotten the exhortation which is addressed to you as sons,
   "MY SON, DO NOT REGARD LIGHTLY THE DISCIPLINE OF THE LORD,
   NOR FAINT WHEN YOU ARE REPROVED BY HIM;
6 FOR THOSE WHOM THE LORD LOVES HE DISCIPLINES,
   AND HE SCOURGES EVERY SON WHOM HE RECEIVES."
7 It is for discipline that you endure; God deals with you as with sons; for what son is there
   whom his father does not discipline?
8 But if you are without discipline, of which all have become partakers, then you are
   illegitimate children and not sons.
9 Furthermore, we had earthly fathers to discipline us, and we respected them; shall we not
   much rather be subject to the Father of spirits, and live?
10 For they disciplined us for a short time as seemed best to them, but He disciplines us for our
   good, so that we may share His holiness.
11 All discipline for the moment seems not to be joyful, but sorrowful; yet to those who have been
   trained by it, afterwards it yields the peaceful fruit of righteousness.
12 Therefore, strengthen the hands that are weak and the knees that are feeble,
13 and make straight paths for your feet, so that the limb which is lame may not be put out of
   joint, but rather be healed.
14 Pursue peace with all men, and the sanctification without which no one will see the Lord.
15 See to it that no one comes short of the grace of God; that no root of bitterness springing up
   causes trouble, and by it many be defiled.

2. What did you learn from marking the word *discipline*? List your insights below. Remember these are God's precepts for life; His truths that will take you victoriously through many a difficult situation.

3. Review the instructions you underlined. What do you see? Think about it.
   Apply it to your life.

How could David, a man after God's own heart, have responded any differently than he did to God's discipline? Remember, God was disciplining David as His child (something it seems David failed to do with Amnon and Absalom). Love the disciplines of your Father, precious one. They are evidence of His love, the certainty that He has a plan, a purpose for you that is not yet complete.

We are not to take the discipline of the Lord lightly. We are not to faint under it. We are instead to "be subject to God"—to not rebel, walk away, say it is too much, not fair. If we do, we jeopardize our Christlikeness and our future, possibly cutting short our lives on this earth.

Sin is not the end of life. Unless God takes us home prematurely, which is possible according to 1 John 5:16-17, we have lessons to learn and a new level of righteousness to be acquired. Our holiness is God's goal.

Don't faint; rather, endure. Pursue holiness—sanctification. God is preparing you to see Him, and He wants you to be holy as He is holy (see Heb. 12). That should encourage you.

Just remember God's grace is sufficient for any and every discipline. And those who are trained by it reap the peaceable fruit of righteousness (Heb. 12:11). Watch what happened to David! We have not yet come to the awesome truth I want us to see, the "previousness" of grace. How it has blessed and encouraged me!

WEEK SIX | DAY THREE
~Swayed by the Deceiver~

Today we need to fast-forward to 2 Samuel 24, where once again David blew it! Despite Joab's warnings, David ordered the registration of the tribes of Israel and Judah. Joab reported that Israel had 800,000 valiant men who drew the sword, and Judah had 500,000—impressive numbers by human standards but not to God. God already knew. According to 1 Chronicles 21:1, although God was angry with Israel, Satan was behind David's decision.

Once again, consequences come. We must never forget that when we sow to the flesh, we reap corruption (see Gal. 6:8).

Let's read 2 Samuel 24:10-17. Once again, let's mark the text. Observing God's Word in this way brings not only a greater focus on truth but it also keeps us from distorting truth. Your most important task in life is to know exactly what God says and to order your thinking and life according to His precepts. This is why you must spend the greater portion of your reading and studying in God's Word rather than in the writings of man. This is the only way you can discover truth for yourself—and believe me, in the times in which we are living, it is imperative that you know truth—that you understand that the Word of God is your plumb line by which you are to measure all you hear and believe.

David was swayed by the Devil—a liar, a deceiver, a murderer, and an accuser who often disguises himself as an angel of light (2 Cor. 11:3,14-15).

1. As you read 2 Samuel 24:10-17:
    * Mark any reference to time or timing with a green circle. If God tells you when something occurs, then He has a purpose in doing it.

    * Double underline in green every geographical location, anything that tells you where.

    * Color every reference to *sin* (doing what is wrong) in brown or mark it as you have done previously.

    * Mark every reference to David, including pronouns and synonyms. It is important to note who—the people—who they are, what they do. As you study inductively, eventually you will train yourself to do this. Marking people simply gets you started.

    * Color-code in yellow everything the Lord said.

REDEEMED

I always mark *heart* in the Bible with a red heart. I do this because the heart/mind is the control center of a person's life. If it is God's heart, I color it yellow; if a good heart, red. If it is desperately wicked, I color it black. If I see the word *hate* I draw a heart, color it black, and put a backslash over it.

2 Samuel 24:10-17, NASB

10 *Now David's heart troubled him after he had numbered the people. So David said to the LORD, "I have sinned greatly in what I have done. But now, O LORD, please take away the iniquity of Your servant, for I have acted very foolishly."*

11 *When David arose in the morning, the word of the LORD came to the prophet Gad, David's seer, saying,*

12 *"Go and speak to David, 'Thus the LORD says, "I am offering you three things; choose for yourself one of them, which I will do to you."'"*

13 *So Gad came to David and told him, and said to him, "Shall seven years of famine come to you in your land? Or will you flee three months before your foes while they pursue you? Or shall there be three days' pestilence in your land? Now consider and see what answer I shall return to Him who sent me."*

14 *Then David said to Gad, "I am in great distress. Let us now fall into the hand of the LORD for His mercies are great, but do not let me fall into the hand of man."*

15 *So the LORD sent a pestilence upon Israel from the morning until the appointed time, and seventy thousand men of the people from Dan to Beersheba died.*

16 *When the angel stretched out his hand toward Jerusalem to destroy it, the LORD relented from the calamity and said to the angel who destroyed the people, "It is enough! Now relax your hand!" And the angel of the LORD was by the threshing floor of Araunah the Jebusite.*

17 *Then David spoke to the LORD when he saw the angel who was striking down the people, and said, "Behold, it is I who have sinned, and it is I who have done wrong; but these sheep, what have they done? Please let Your hand be against me and against my father's house."*

When you observe the Word of God, ask yourself the 5 W's and an H: who, what, when, where, why, and how.

Now take time to think about what you have just observed. Our lives are so rushed that we often don't take time to meditate on God's Word. How sorry we are going to be someday! How will we explain to God that we didn't have time for His very words of life—words that give us the answer to all of life's questions? words that direct our steps and lead us in paths of righteousness?

2. What was happening in 2 Samuel 24:10-17? If someone were to ask you to summarize this incident, how would you do it in three sentences or less? Write your summary here.

You probably included the fact that God gave David some options when it came to his punishment. How many options did David have? (I am asking this so you can do something that will help you when studying the Bible inductively. Learn to number lists in the text, marking *1, 2, 3,* and so forth. You can spot lists quickly, remember them better, and spot something important.)

3. Number the list of options in verse 13.

Let's finish 2 Samuel 24 because the facts of this event carry incredible weight, even for today.

4. Once again observe the text by marking
   David
   Altar
   Threshing floor, double underlining it in green

2 Samuel 24:18-25, NASB

18 *So Gad came to David that day and said to him, "Go up, erect an altar to the LORD on the threshing floor of Araunah the Jebusite."*

19 *David went up according to the word of Gad, just as the LORD had commanded.*

20 *Araunah looked down and saw the king and his servants crossing over toward him; and Araunah went out and bowed his face to the ground before the king.*

21 *Then Araunah said, "Why has my lord the king come to his servant?" And David said, "To buy the threshing floor from you, in order to build an altar to the LORD, that the plague may be held back from the people."*

22 *Araunah said to David, "Let my lord the king take and offer up what is good in his sight. Look, the oxen for the burnt offering, the threshing sledges and the yokes of the oxen for the wood.*

23 *"Everything, O king, Araunah gives to the king." And Araunah said to the king, "May the LORD your God accept you."*

24 *However, the king said to Araunah, "No, but I will surely buy it from you for a price, for I will not offer burnt offerings to the LORD my God which cost me nothing." So David bought the threshing floor and the oxen for fifty shekels of silver.*

25 *David built there an altar to the LORD and offered burnt offerings and peace offerings. Thus the LORD was moved by prayer for the land, and the plague was held back from Israel.*

Now, beloved, although I'd like to stretch you with more study today, I will restrain myself. (It's just that I get so excited, and I don't want you to miss anything! Life is too short.)

5. List everything you learned from double underlining the references to the threshing floor. By the way, make sure you know where "the floor" is—what city. Look at verse 16 in the text on page 126. Underline the location and include it in your list.

Well, beloved, that is it for today. Did you learn anything you can apply to your life—anything about the Lord, about yourself, about sin? Write it down and then take it to the Lord in prayer. Or, better still, write out your prayer. It will be good to come back and read it again.

WEEK SIX | DAY FOUR

His Crossroad of Grace

God is righteous, isn't He? You've certainly seen it in David's life. God must judge sin. It cannot be overlooked. His holiness and righteousness is manifested in His just judgment of sin. Yet I wonder how many really believe this. Do you?

David certainly did. You've seen it in David's lifestyle as you've studied with dear Priscilla and Beth. You saw him live in the fear of God—respecting God, trusting God, honoring God as God. David was willing not to rush the will of God, not to take matters into his own hands and usurp God's timing in delivering the kingdom into his promised hands. David could have taken Saul's life—he had the opportunity—but he left it to God. This is the beauty of studying 1 and 2 Samuel precept upon precept. You see these details for yourself. They then become yours!

When David sinned, you saw his respect for the character of God. David honored God's holiness by never murmuring or disputing God's discipline. David, an Old Testament king, lived in the grace of God and we are about to see the amazing prescience—or as I like to say previousness of that grace. Remember, grace is favor, unearned, unmerited. It is kindness from God. Grace is because God is! Grace is also power, power perfected in our weaknesses for when I am weak then I am strong. Why? Because I am relying on God rather than myself; therefore, it is a crossroad that will take us deeper still, if we'll travel that way. Grace takes us past our failures and our foibles.

I am so excited to have you see it. It's an awesome way to bring our brief six-week study on David to a close. When I studied God's Word comparing Scripture with Scripture and allowing the Spirit of God to lead me and guide me into His truth, I could hardly contain myself when the Lord opened the eyes of my understanding. He used it in a precious way to comfort my hurting heart. Oh, may He achieve a special purpose in your life as He opens the eyes of your understanding.

I want us to go back to where we began last week with David's sin with Bathsheba and look at what happened after the unnamed child of their illicit union died.

1. Turn in your Bible to 2 Samuel 12:23-25. When was Solomon conceived? (Pay attention to time words—"then.")

Jedidiah means "beloved of the Lord." Isn't that neat!

2. Now according to the sequence of 2 Samuel 12, what happened after Solomon was conceived? Read 2 Samuel 12:26-31.

Good. Now let's go to 1 Chronicles. It's interesting that this book never mentions the sin of David against Bathsheba and her husband Uriah. However, it does mention that when it was time for kings to go to war, David stayed in Jerusalem (1 Chron. 20:1).

The end of 2 Samuel, the Book of 1 Kings, and then 1 Chronicles all cover similar material. However, each of the books has different purposes, being written at different times. Chronicles was written after Samuel and Kings as a preparation for Israel's return to the land after their 70 years of captivity.

3. Quickly read 1 Chronicles 20:1-8 and 21:1,28-30 so you can see the timing and sequence of events. (Ornan is another spelling of Araunah in 2 Sam. 24.) What does it parallel that you have already studied?

4. Now read 1 Chronicles 22:1-13 below. As you do, mark the following:
   * Color every reference to the **house of the Lord** dark blue.
   * Mark every reference to **preparation**. Color it green or the color of your preference.
   * Put a green circle over all references to time or sequence of time.
   * Color every reference to Solomon in a color of your choosing.
   * Mark the **word of the Lord** with an open book like this 📖

1 Chronicles 22:1-13, NASB

1   Then David said, "This is the house of the LORD God, and this is the altar of burnt offering for Israel."
2   So David gave orders to gather the foreigners who were in the land of Israel, and he set stonecutters to hew out stones to build the house of God.
3   David prepared large quantities of iron to make the nails for the doors of the gates and for the clamps, and more bronze than could be weighed;
4   and timbers of cedar logs beyond number, for the Sidonians and Tyrians brought large quantities of cedar timber to David.
5   David said, "My son Solomon is young and inexperienced, and the house that is to be built for the LORD shall be exceedingly magnificent, famous and glorious throughout all lands. Therefore now I will make preparation for it." So David made ample preparations before his death.
6   Then he called for his son Solomon, and charged him to build a house for the LORD God of Israel.
7   David said to Solomon, "My son, I had intended to build a house to the name of the LORD my God.

8 *"But the word of the LORD came to me, saying, 'You have shed much blood and have waged great wars; you shall not build a house to My name, because you have shed so much blood on the earth before Me.*

9 *'Behold, a son will be born to you, who shall be a man of rest; and I will give him rest from all his enemies on every side; for his name shall be Solomon, and I will give peace and quiet to Israel in his days.*

10 *'He shall build a house for My name, and he shall be My son and I will be his father; and I will establish the throne of his kingdom over Israel forever.'*

11 *"Now, my son, the LORD be with you that you may be successful, and build the house of the LORD your God just as He has spoken concerning you.*

12 *"Only the LORD give you discretion and understanding, and give you charge over Israel, so that you may keep the law of the LORD your God.*

13 *"Then you will prosper, if you are careful to observe the statutes and the ordinances which the LORD commanded Moses concerning Israel. Be strong and courageous, do not fear nor be dismayed.*

Wonderful! List below what you learned from marking the references to the *house of the Lord*. Only what the Scriptures say—nothing more, nothing less.

5. What did you learn from marking **preparation**?

6. What did you learn from marking **Solomon**? Carefully list your insights.

We are making progress. You'll soon see where we are going, so hangeth thou in there. I am so very proud of you for wanting to discover truth for yourself.

7. According to the text you just observed, when was David told that Solomon would build the house of the Lord?

If you want to really appreciate the sovereign grace of God, understand it deeper still, and then live accordingly. Look at 2 Samuel 7:1-13 in your Bible. Don't skip this. Read those verses. In fact, read the entire chapter if you have time. It is one of the most important chapters in the entire Old Testament. Read it first. Then answer the following questions:

8. What did David want to do?

9. Whom did David tell this to?

10. What was the prophet's first response?

11. What did God tell David about his desire? Why couldn't he have it?

12. According to verse 11, what was God going to do?

13. How long was this kingdom going to last?

What you have just read and is explained even more in verses 14-29—is the Davidic Covenant. While the word *covenant* is not used in 2 Samuel 7, 2 Chronicles 13:5 calls it a covenant. A covenant is a solemn, binding agreement that God watches over.

The Davidic Covenant lays out the genealogy of the Messiah, the Christ. The Messiah must be a descendant of David. From this point on in the Old Testament, this promise or covenant is referred to again and again. This is why the New Testament opens with the genealogy of Jesus as given in Matthew 1. It establishes Jesus' birthright as the son of David to the throne of Israel, which in turn makes Jesus King! King of the Jews. King of kings. You see the same in the Book of Acts as Jesus is validated as Messiah and again in the introduction to the Book of Romans, the constitution of our faith. But this is not what I want you to see and delight in—it is something else.

What is it? It's the chronology—the timing of God's word to David that he would have a son born to him who would not only sit on David's throne but would build the house of the Lord.

14. Open your Bible again. Depending on the Bible you have, chapters and content within chapters are marked according to themes. Content-wise it might look something like this:

CHAPTER 6	David Moves the Ark to the City of David (Jerusalem)
CHAPTER 7	God Establishes David's Throne Forever
CHAPTER 8	David Subdues Nations with the Lord's Help
CHAPTER 9	David's *"Hesed"* to Mephibosheth *(Hesed* is lovingkindness, a covenant term)
CHAPTER 10	David Defeats Ammonites, Arameans
CHAPTER 11	David Takes Bathsheba, Kills Uriah
CHAPTER 12	David's Fourfold Judgment, Birth of Solomon
CHAPTER 13	Absalom Kills Amnon and Flees

Stop and think this through.

15. According to what you have read and marked in 1 Chronicles 22, when was David told about the birth of Solomon?

16. When was he told his name?

17. When did David take Bathsheba in adultery? Was it before or after God told David he would have a son who would sit on his throne forever and build a house for the Lord?

18. Do you see the previousness of God's grace?

Before David ever sinned with Bathsheba, God knew what would happen. Just as before God ever created the world, God knew Adam and Eve would sin. God knew death would enter the world through their sin, and in His grace God made provision for man's sin—the Father, Son, and Holy Spirit had a plan for the redemption of mankind made in their image. Jesus would be the Lamb of God, slain before the foundation of the world! Salvation has always been by grace, because God in all His holiness, righteousness, and justice is also a God of love, a God of grace. Where sin abounded, grace abounded even more. It's lavish, extravagant grace. It is previous grace! So shall we sin that more grace might come? God forbid! Grace is not license to sin; rather, it is power not to sin and love that covers it when we do.

First Chronicles lets us know that before Solomon was ever born, he was named by God and ordained to build the house of the Lord. And where would Solomon build it? Watch this!

19. Go to 2 Chronicles 3:1 and see where it was built. Write it down right here.

If you understand the Bible, you understand that the temple mount, where the temple of Solomon was built, belongs to the Israelites, the Jews—not the Muslims. It was purchased by David the king in the city of the king, Jerusalem, where God put His name. This is a biblical worldview on this issue!

Oh, beloved of God, do you see it? Do you understand it? This is the prescient grace of God. What was David's is yours—appropriate it, walk in it, abide in it. No matter what you have done, you will be able to go deeper still. If you are alive, there is a future; there is hope because there is God. We will look at this future tomorrow.

WEEK SIX | DAY FIVE

Celebrating God's Grace

Was that it for David? Would he never do anything great for God? Was his sin the end of his service? Was he simply to wait out the years of the fourfold consequence of his grave transgressions against God? Was he simply to deteriorate, decay, and rust out? Were his final years to be spent in contemplation of his sin? Remembering his transgressions, thinking of what-ifs and if-onlys?

1. Let's return to 1 Chronicles 22 and observe the rest of the chapter and the first verse of chapter 23. As you read it, once again mark the words you did previously: *house* (sanctuary), *prepared, Solomon*.

1 Chronicles 22:14–23:1, NASB

14 *"Now behold, with great pains I have prepared for the house of the LORD 100,000 talents of gold and 1,000,000 talents of silver, and bronze and iron beyond weight, for they are in great quantity; also timber and stone I have prepared, and you may add to them.*

15 *"Moreover, there are many workmen with you, stonecutters and masons of stone and carpenters, and all men who are skillful in every kind of work.*

16 *"Of the gold, the silver and the bronze and the iron there is no limit. Arise and work, and may the LORD be with you."*

17 *David also commanded all the leaders of Israel to help his son Solomon, saying,*

18 *"Is not the LORD your God with you? And has He not given you rest on every side? For He has given the inhabitants of the land into my hand, and the land is subdued before the LORD and before His people.*

19 *"Now set your heart and your soul to seek the LORD your God; arise, therefore, and build the sanctuary of the LORD God, so that you may bring the ark of the covenant of the LORD and the holy vessels of God into the house that is to be built for the name of the LORD."*

23:1 *Now when David reached old age, he made his son Solomon king over Israel.*

2. What did you learn from marking *prepared*?

3. What was David being permitted to do?

4. At what time of life was David doing this?

5. Was life over for David? Give the reason for your answer.

Now let's go to 1 Chronicles 28–29, two glorious chapters. We will take them one at a time.

6. Read 1 Chronicles 28:1-9,13-21 and mark the following:
   * Color all the references to **David** in light blue.
   * Mark the references to the **house of the Lord**.
   * Mark **plan**. The word **pattern** is also used.
   * Mark **heart**.
   * Put a green circle over all references to **time**.

1 Chronicles 28:1-9,13-21, NASB

1 *Now David assembled at Jerusalem all the officials of Israel, the princes of the tribes, and the commanders of the divisions that served the king, and the commanders of thousands, and the commanders of hundreds, and the overseers of all the property and livestock belonging to the king and his sons, with the officials and the mighty men, even all the valiant men.*

2 *Then King David rose to his feet and said, "Listen to me, my brethren and my people; I had intended to build a permanent home for the ark of the covenant of the LORD and for the footstool of our God. So I had made preparations to build it.*

3 *"But God said to me, "You shall not build a house for My name because you are a man of war and have shed blood.'*

4 *"Yet, the LORD, the God of Israel, chose me from all the house of my father to be king over Israel forever. For He has chosen Judah to be a leader; and in the house of Judah, my father's house, and among the sons of my father He took pleasure in me to make me king over all Israel.*

5 *"Of all my sons (for the LORD has given me many sons), He has chosen my son Solomon to sit on the throne of the kingdom of the LORD over Israel.*

6 *"He said to me, 'Your son Solomon is the one who shall build My house and My courts; for I have chosen him to be a son to Me, and I will be a father to him.*

7 *'I will establish his kingdom forever if he resolutely performs My commandments and My ordinances, as is done now.'*

8 *"So now, in the sight of all Israel, the assembly of the LORD, and in the hearing of our God, observe and seek after all the commandments of the LORD your God so that you may possess the good land and bequeath it to your sons after you forever.*

9 *"As for you, my son Solomon, know the God of your father, and serve Him with a whole heart and a willing mind; for the LORD searches all hearts, and understands every intent of the thoughts. If you seek Him, He will let you find Him; but if you forsake Him, He will reject you forever."*

* * * * * * * *

13 *also for the divisions of the priests and the Levites and for all the work of the service of the house of the LORD and for all the utensils of service in the house of the LORD;*

14 *for the golden utensils, the weight of gold for all utensils for every kind of service; for the silver utensils, the weight of silver for all utensils for every kind of service;*

15 *and the weight of gold for the golden lampstands and their golden lamps, with the weight of each lampstand and its lamps; and the weight of silver for the silver lampstands, with the weight of each lampstand and its lamps according to the use of each lampstand;*

16 *and the gold by weight for the tables of showbread, for each table; and silver for the silver tables;*

17 *and the forks, the basins, and the pitchers of pure gold; and for the golden bowls with the weight for each bowl; and for the silver bowls with the weight for each bowl;*

18 *and for the altar of incense refined gold by weight; and gold for the model of the chariot, even the cherubim that spread out their wings and covered the ark of the covenant of the LORD.*

19 *"All this," said David, "the LORD made me understand in writing by His hand upon me, all the details of this pattern."*

20 *Then David said to his son Solomon, "Be strong and courageous, and act; do not fear nor be dismayed, for the LORD God, my God, is with you. He will not fail you nor forsake you until all the work for the service of the house of the LORD is finished.*

21 *"Now behold, there are the divisions of the priests and the Levites for all the service of the house of God, and every willing man of any skill will be with you in all the work for all kinds of service. The officials also and all the people will be entirely at your command."*

7. What was David's future like, even bearing the disciplines of the Lord? Was there life after sin? grace to cover the sin, power to go on? Look at the words you marked. What was David allowed to do?

How awesome was that? Verse 19, "by His hand upon me," brought tears to my eyes. How special Finally, let's look at some select verses from 1 Chronicles 29. Read the first three verses in your Bible so you'll have them pictured in your mind. When you come to "with all my ability" underline it.

Do you see—David's zeal, his passion to serve God, did not wane with age or failure. In verse 3 you see David giving even more—he didn't stop giving to the house of his God.

Neither did David lose his joy.

8. Read the following Scripture. Mark every reference to:
    Joy and/or *delight*
    Ability

1 Chronicles 29:1-9

1 *Then King David said to the entire assembly, "My son Solomon, whom alone God has chosen, is still young and inexperienced and the work is great; for the temple is not for man, but for the LORD God.*

2 *"Now with all my ability I have provided for the house of my God the gold for the things of gold, and the silver for the things of silver, and the bronze for the things of bronze, the iron for the things of iron, and wood for the things of wood, onyx stones and inlaid stones, stones of antimony and stones of various colors, and all kinds of precious stones and alabaster in abundance.*

3 *"Moreover, in my delight in the house of my God, the treasure I have of gold and silver, I give to the house of my God, over and above all that I have already provided for the holy temple,*

4 *namely, 3,000 talents of gold, of the gold of Ophir, and 7,000 talents of refined silver, to overlay the walls of the buildings;*

5 *of gold for the things of gold and of silver for the things of silver, that is, for all the work done by the craftsmen. Who then is willing to consecrate himself this day to the LORD?"*

6 *Then the rulers of the fathers' households, and the princes of the tribes of Israel, and the commanders of thousands and of hundreds, with the overseers over the king's work, offered willingly;*

7 *and for the service for the house of God they gave 5,000 talents and 10,000 darics of gold, and 10,000 talents of silver, and 18,000 talents of brass, and 100,000 talents of iron.*

8 *Whoever possessed precious stones gave them to the treasury of the house of the LORD, in care of Jehiel the Gershonite.*

9 *Then the people rejoiced because they had offered so willingly, for they made their offering to the LORD with a whole heart, and King David also rejoiced greatly.*

Look at the words you just marked. What does this tell you about David "after sin" and repentance? As you answer this question, just remember if David had sinned but had not repented with a godly sorrow and confessed his sin, these things would not have been true in his life.

9. The following Scripture gives you insight into David's heart toward God. As you read it, color yellow every reference to the Lord.

10 *So David blessed the LORD in the sight of all the assembly; and David said, "Blessed are You, O LORD God of Israel our father, forever and ever.*

11 *"Yours, O LORD, is the greatness and the power and the glory and the victory and the majesty, indeed everything that is in the heavens and the earth; Yours is the dominion, O LORD, and You exalt Yourself as head over all.*

12 *"Both riches and honor come from You, and You rule over all, and in Your hand is power and might; and it lies in Your hand to make great and to strengthen everyone.*

13 *"Now therefore, our God, we thank You, and praise Your glorious name.*

14 *"But who am I and who are my people that we should be able to offer as generously as this? For all things come from You, and from Your hand we have given You.*

15 *"For we are sojourners before You, and tenants, as all our fathers were; our days on the earth are like a shadow, and there is no hope.*

16 *"O LORD our God, all this abundance that we have provided to build You a house for Your holy name, it is from Your hand, and all is Yours.*

17 *"Since I know, O my God, that You try the heart and delight in uprightness, I, in the integrity of my heart, have willingly offered all these things; so now with joy I have seen Your people, who are present here, make their offerings willingly to You.*

18 *"O LORD, the God of Abraham, Isaac and Israel, our fathers, preserve this forever in the intentions of the heart of Your people, and direct their heart to You;*

19 *"and give to my son Solomon a perfect heart to keep Your commandments, Your testimonies and Your statutes, and to do them all, and to build the temple, for which I have made provision."*

20 *Then David said to all the assembly, "Now bless the LORD your God." And all the assembly blessed the LORD, the God of their fathers, and bowed low and did homage to the LORD and to the king.*

10. As we bring our study to a close, list what you learned from marking the references to the Lord. You will find it well worth your time.

When David finished his prayer, he told the people to bless the Lord their God. May I suggest you take a few minutes to do the same? Read your list aloud and then spend a few minutes blessing God for who He is. The Scriptures tell us He inhabits the praises of His people. May you sense His presence.

First Chronicles 29:28 tells us David "died in a ripe old age, full of days, riches and honor; and his son Solomon reigned in his place."

Oh the grace of God—the lavish, extravagant, previous grace of God! And what if David had missed it by not believing God is who He says He is and aligning his life and his response to sin and God's judgment accordingly? What if David had not gone deeper still?

*   *   *   *   *   *   *   *   *

When David finished his prayer, it says the people "ate and drank that day before the Lord with great gladness" (1 Chron. 29:22). Have you thought of having your own party now that you have finished your six-week study? It is a cause to celebrate and an opportunity to share what God has taught you through this study.

And what about you, beloved student of God's Word, will you go deeper still with me? By the grace of God, I'm going there for as long as I have left…..

ANOINTED
TRANSFORMED
REDEEMED

LEADER GUIDE

Welcome to a study of the life of David with Priscilla, Beth, and Kay. This guide has been prepared to help you plan and lead the study. It includes help for planning and promoting and a session-by-session guide.

Provide each participant with the book. Activities encourage personal inter-action. The study includes six weeks of content—two by each of the authors—with a final meeting to discuss the last week's work and to celebrate, the group will last seven weeks. Each week's material includes five daily lessons, requiring about 30 minutes to read and respond. You can adjust the time to fit your group needs.

In the small-group portion of sessions, participants share and discuss what God has taught them from His Word. Small-group sessions build fellowship and relationships, encourage accountability, and multiply the

benefits of the study. Women draw closer as they share their thoughts, personal experiences, needs, and prayer concerns.

In the large-group women watch the video teaching. Leadership suggestions in this guide reflect the following schedule:

Child-care (15 min. before session)
Large group—welcome and worship (15 min.)
Large group—video presentation (40 min.)
Break and to small groups (variable time)
Small groups—discussion of the video and past week's work, closing assignment prayer

This guide offers suggestions for leading your group. Adapt it to meet the needs of the women in your church and community. Each small-group leader may also adapt the suggestions to her own style or preferences.

Choosing Leaders

If you have 12 or fewer women you need only one leader for both the large- and small-group. If more women are involved, divide into groups of 8 to 12. You will need a leader for the large group as well as for each small group.

Large-group leader: responsibilities include
• providing administrative leadership
• scheduling and promoting the study
• enlisting small-group leaders
• ordering resources and distributing books
• leading the weekly large-group sessions

Small-group facilitators: work with 8 to 12 women to guide discussion.
• stay in contact and encourage their group
• lead small-group prayer time and pray regularly for participants
• guide discussion during small-group time
• follow up on ministry needs

Small-group leaders can use the following suggestions to facilitate discussion.

Before the Session
• Pray for members by name each week.
• Do your homework.
• Pray for God to guide you as you facilitate.
• Arrange chairs in a circle.

During the Session
• Greet members and start on time.
• Share prayer requests and pray.
• Encourage voluntary sharing. Invite everyone to participate, but make sure no one feels compelled to share personal information beyond her comfort level.
• Be flexible. If women are engaged in meaningful discussion, don't force them to move on just to finish the agenda. On the other hand, don't let one or two women bog down the discussion.
• Share some of your own thoughts and feelings to facilitate discussion. Your example can help women be vulnerable without revealing too many intimate details.

• Whatever women share, show compassion, concern, and support.
• Keep the discussion focused.
• Listen actively by looking at each woman as she speaks and affirm her for sharing.
• Be prepared to lead a participant to faith in Christ.
• End on time. If you see that women want to continue the discussion, consider exchanging e-mail comments during the week.
• Encourage members to do their home study.

After the Session
• Encourage women and follow up on any ministry needs.
• Evaluate the session. Pray for insight and sensitivity to God's Spirit and women's needs.
• Prepare daily for the next session.

Planning Steps

The following steps are suggested to assist the large-group leader.
1. Enlist the support of the pastor.
2. Talk with women in your church. Take a poll to discover whether the study should be offered during the day, the evening, or both.
3. Schedule time on the church calendar.
4. Offer child care, if possible.
5. Estimate the number of participants and order books four to six weeks in advance. If members pay at least part of the cost of their books, they are more likely to attend faithfully and to complete their home study. If you charge for the books, arrange for scholarship funds as needed.
6. Reserve rooms and electronic equipment.
7. Promote the study. Target women in your community who are interested in Bible study. Church bulletins, newsletters, handouts, posters, fliers at Mothers' Day Out, announcements in worship services and in Sunday School classes, phone calls, and word of mouth are excellent and inexpensive ways to promote the study.
8. Pray that God will involve the members He desires and that He will validate this study with His presence activity in members' lives.

Session 1

Before the Session

1. Pray for group members.
2. Read about the three authors.
3. Provide name tags.

Prepare name tags in advance. On each name tag, have one of the words: *Anointed*, *Transformed*, or *Redeemed*. Mix the tags so women who arrive in groups will get different name tags. Use the tags to divide women into three groups. If you need to divide further use different color tags. Use these name tags to form the same small groups for the entire seven weeks. Provide markers for name tags.

4. Have books ready to distribute.
5. Provide paper and pens or pencils.
6. For the large group meeting place, make three large banners, each with one of these words: *Anointed, Transformed, Redeemed*. Display all three during this session, then display only the relevant banner. For the last session, display all three again.

During the Session (Large Group)

1. Welcome women as they arrive. Ask them to make name tags.
2. Ask women to find someone they don't know well and share one reason they have come to this Bible study.
3. Introduce yourself and other leaders. Create a casual, nonthreatening atmosphere. Suggest that they pray for one another throughout the next six weeks.
4. Introduce the first video by saying that David was chosen by God. Direct women to turn to the viewer guide for week one in their books. Make sure women have pens or pencils. Show the first video session. View the first video by Priscilla Shirer.
5. Direct women to their small groups.

Small Group

1. Invite women to brainstorm all that they can remember about David. As they call out answers, list the events of David's life and characteristics about him on a chalkboard, whiteboard, or large sheets of paper. You may wish to refer to Priscilla's time line on page 14.

2. Explain that this study will focus on some aspects of David's life. Say: *Paul preached that God said, "I have found David the son of Jesse, a man after My heart"* (Acts 13:22). Ask: *In what ways do you think David had a heart like God's?* List responses. Suggest they listen and watch throughout the study for ways David had a heart like God's.

3. Discuss the group discussion questions from the viewer guide (p. 9).

4. Note that David knew who and whose he was. Ask women to share in small groups of three or four how their lives are defined by other people or roles (husbands or boyfriends, children, parents, friends, jobs). Ask them how their relationship to God defines their lives.

5. Point out that God wanted the ark to be in Jerusalem as a symbol of God's presence. The ark contained the tablets of the Ten Commandments and samples of manna, and it traveled with the people wherever they went. Ask women to envision a personal ark, a box or container of some kind, that represents their relationship with God. What real or imaginary items would they place in their ark?

6. David faced opposition throughout his life. His father brought him last to Samuel to be considered as king. His brothers ridiculed him when he visited them on the battlefield. Saul tried to have him killed. He fought wars to unite and build the kingdom of Israel. Ask the women what opposition or barriers they face or have faced in trying to do what they believe God wants them to do. After women have shared, point out that some may have faced obstacles or opposition in making time for this Bible study. Ask women to pray for one another that opposition and obstacles will not keep them from doing their study each day or for coming to the next six sessions.

7. Close in prayer. Thank God for the lessons women will learn from David. Thank Him for anointing all those who call Him Lord.

Session 2

Before the Session

1. Display a few handmade crafts or personal treasures such as a quilt or a child's art.
2. For small groups, draw a time line of David's life on the whiteboard or chalkboard.
3. Provide name tags, paper and pens.
4. Make a *Wanted* poster with a mirror on it and the words: *Wanted* (above the mirror) and below the mirror: *Perfect* with an X through the word, then *Passionate Women*. Or write the words on a large mirror and display it in the room. Place this poster or mirror near the door while women are watching the video.

During the Session (Large Group)

1. As women arrive, ask them to gather in groups of three or four and talk about a special handmade item in their homes.
2. When everyone has arrived and had opportunity to participate, call the large group together and pray.
3. Tell about the handcrafted items you have made. Invite a few women to share about the items they discussed. Point out that many years ago "handmade" or "homemade" meant you couldn't afford to buy something. Now something handmade is valued because the maker invested time and love in the project. Similarly, handpicked items are valued because they are carefully selected. Introduce the week by saying that David was "handpicked by God," as are believers today.

Small Group

1. Ask for questions from the week's work.
2. Suggested questions for discussion:
   - How do you feel knowing that you, like David, have been "handpicked" by God?
   - How does realizing that God chose you affect your relationship with Him?
   - How does or should being handpicked affect your decision making?
3. Share in small groups of three or four: *You were picked by God for a purpose. What is it?*

4. Ask women to draw their personal time lines with significant dates such as birth, new birth (salvation), major decisions or turning points in life, times they were chosen for a particular role or task. Invite volunteers to share times when God was clearly directing in the decisions they made. Ask if they ever felt that they were being "handpicked" for a job that was greater than they could do alone.
5. Based on content from day two, lead a discussion about David and the ark.
6. Conclude this part by saying that usually election or selection means, "winning" for one person losing for another. If one person is elected to public office, another is defeated. If one woman is chosen for a promotion, others who wanted the job did not. But in the kingdom of God, all are handpicked by God.
7. Pray that because women feel loved as handpicked for kingdom service that their lives will be filled with joy.

Large Group

1. Direct women to turn to the viewer guide for week two. Make sure women have pens or pencils. Show the second video session.
2. Discuss the group discussion questions.
3. Ask if any of the women have questions about the video. Invite them to recall and comment on what connected with them.
4. Point out that during their studies they will be looking at opposition when they try to do what God calls them to do as well as access to God, directions from God, and the promise of supernatural results.
5. End with prayer asking God to bless this group of women in the coming week.
6. Refer to the *Wanted* poster before women leave the room. Ask each woman to look closely at the poster (in the mirror) as she leaves. Say that God wants women to put their passions to work in His kingdom this week. Tell them you will be praying for them as they serve God this week.

Session 3

Before the Session

1. Display a photograph of a family or church member who is known for loving God and for having a close faith walk with Him.
2. Enlist a woman in advance to pray at the beginning of the large-group session.
3. Continue to display the *Wanted* poster or mirror.

During the Session (Large Group)

1. As women arrive, ask them to gather in small groups and to tell about a family member, church member, or close friend whose close walk with God has been an inspiration to them.
2. Call them together and tell about the person you have chosen whose faith made a difference in your life.
3. Share church prayer concerns and ask for additional concerns. Call on the woman you have enlisted to pray.
4. Direct women to their small groups.

Small Group

1. Ask women if they have questions about the week's work. Invite them to turn through week two and to read Scriptures that blessed them and to say what impact that passage had.
2. Ask: *When Samuel went to Jesse's house to find Israel's new king, why did Jesse not bring in David? What did God see that Jesse, and perhaps Samuel at first, did not see?*
3. Write on the board: *Anointing—a divine enablement to accomplish divine tasks.* Ask women to share a time when God has given them a God-sized task that they could do only with God's help.
4. Ask these and other questions:
   - What opposition did David face?
   - How did David handle opposition?
   - How did being selected by God make a difference in David's life?
   - How did God use ordinary events to prepare David for extraordinary roles?
   - What opposition have you faced when you were trying to do God's bidding?
   - How is life in Christ "abundant" even when facing opposition?
   - How did David's role and God's directions change over time?
   - How has God guided you in different directions over time?
5. Brainstorm David's responsibilities. Write them on the board as women name them. He also had many benefits. Write those as well. Then ask women to list responsibilities women have, both general and specific.
6. Remind women that David wrote many of the psalms. Read Psalm 103:2.
7. Ask women to say eyes-open sentence praises to God naming specific benefits of their love relationship with Him.
8. Move to large group to view video 3.

Large Group

1. Direct them to turn to the viewing guide on page 58-59. Show the video.
2. Discuss the Group Discussion Questions from the viewer guide.
3. Ask women in small groups of three or four to share a time when they have felt they had gone as far as they could go and could go no farther because of devastation, fatigue, or a feeling of hopelessness or inadequacy.
4. Calling women back together ask them how God helped them to keep going even when they thought they could not.
5. Point out that in the midst of our inability to continue, when we must rely on God because we are inadequate, God often chooses that time to transform us. Tell them they will learn more about God's transformation as they study in the coming week.
6. Pray, thanking God for women who have been transformed by His power and grace.

Session 4

Before the Session
1. Display a photograph of one or more people who had a role in either leading you to Christ, helping you grow as a believer, or in calling out your gifts.
2. Enlist a woman in advance to pray at the beginning of the large group session.

During the Session (Large Group)
1. As women arrive, ask them to gather in small groups and to tell about people who were instrumental in bringing them to Jesus Christ, helping them grow as believers, or in calling out your gifts.
2. When women have arrived and had opportunity to participate, call them together and tell about the person you have chosen who helped you come to Christ, grow as a Christian, or find areas of passion in your life that enabled you to serve God.
3. Share church prayer concerns and ask for additional concerns. Call on the woman you have enlisted to pray.
4. Direct women to their small groups.

Small Group
1. Discuss week 3 asking questions such as:
   - What is the Davidic Covenant?
   - What good idea did David have?
   - Why did Nathan go along with David's idea?
   - Why was the good idea not a God idea?
   - How did David learn that God did not approve of his idea?
   - Was God angry? How did He respond?
   - What made David afraid?
   - What made David angry?
   - What verses can you recall from Psalms that reflect some of David's experiences studied this week?
2. Ask women to turn to each other and share answers to these questions:
   - Have you ever had a good idea that turned out not to be a God idea?
   - What happened?

- Are you more likely to react with anger or fear to a frustrating situation?
- Where is God when you are dealing with these emotions?
- What verses from Psalms have helped you when you have faced difficult and emotional times with life and with God?
- Has God used difficult circumstances in your past to lead you to minister to another person in similar circumstances?

3. Calling women back together in the small group, ask:
   - How do Christians today discern whether an idea is a good idea or a God idea?
   - What Scriptures have you found helpful when you are dealing with making a decision and trying to discern where God is leading?

Large Group
1. Assemble the large group for the video. Direct them to the viewer guide on page 78-79.
2. Discuss the group discussion questions.
3. Write on the board the words "Wholehearted obedience."
4. Ask women in small groups of three or four to share a time when they knew they were not being obedient to God. How did they feel? Then ask them to tell about a time when they were doing their best to be obedient to God. How did they feel?
5. Tell women they will look again at anger, fear, and pain in this week's studies, but they will move past all of that to see God's plans and His promises. Encourage them to remain faithful in continuing their studies in the coming week.
6. Pray, asking God to bless these women who have faced the challenges of hurt and pain, disappointment, anger, and fear. Ask God to reveal His plans and promises to them as they spend time in His Word in the coming week.

Session 5

Before the Session

1. Display a photograph of a child in your family making a face or download from the Internet one or more photographs of people making faces. You may project one face or create a PowerPoint slide show of the faces.

2. Enlist a woman in advance to pray at the beginning of the large group session.

During the Session (Large Group)

1. As women arrive, ask them to gather in groups of three or four and tell about the last time they pouted or whined. Or ask them to describe a time they did this as a child. Keep it light and have fun with this.

2. When women have arrived and had time to participate, call them together and remind them that no matter how much we pout, our heavenly Father expects obedience. Explain that as they review session 4 in groups, they will deal with pain, disappointment, and even devastation, but they will always come back to obedience because God made clear that obedience is His choice.

3. Share church prayer concerns and ask for additional concerns. Call on the woman you have enlisted to pray.

4. Direct women to their small groups.

Small Group

1. Ask women if they have any questions from their study in week 4.

2. Invite women to share points from week 4 that were significant to them.

3. Ask women to turn through week 4 in their books and to find and share Scripture verses that were meaningful to them during their studies of the past week.

4. Write on the board, "Wholehearted Obedience." Discuss week 4 asking these and other questions:
   - What obstacles did David face in moving from devastation to obedience?
   - What kinds of things lead women away from obedience?

- What kinds of consequences does sin always have?
- How does God's forgiveness differ from sin's consequences?
- What is the difference in reading Scripture to see how it applies to me and reading it to see what it reveals about God?
- How are obedience to God and relationship with God connected?
- How are obedience to God and worship connected?
- What are the differences between public worship and private worship?
- What are some dangers of public worship?
- Explain what the author means by this statement: "Let's have the courage to see the fulfillment of God's promises."

5. Direct women to large group to view video 5.

Large Group

1. In the large group before viewing the video, introduce Kay Arthur. Ask women to turn to the viewing guide for week 5 (p. 98).

2. After the video return to small groups.

Small Group

1. Write on the board the word, *Redeemed*.

2. Ask women in small groups of three or four to share their salvation experiences. Be ready to talk with anyone who does not know Jesus as Lord and Savior.

3. Explain to women that during the next two weeks they will learn from David's sin and restoration of his relationship with God. Point out that people who are saved still sin, and as they have learned, sin has consequences. But they are still saved, and God still forgives.

4. Pray, asking God to bless these women being redeemed by God's grace. Thank God for His unmerited favor in forgiving us when we sin and come back to Him in repentance.

Session 6

Before the Session
1. Project on the screen an image of a busy intersection or of divergent trails.
2. Enlist a woman in advance to pray at the beginning of the large group session.

During the Session
1. As women arrive, ask them to gather in small groups to discuss crossroads or decisions they made that day, and how different the day might have been if they had made some different choices.

    Option: Read aloud the book *If You Give a Girl a Bible* by Andy Holmes (Kregel KidZone). The book is similar to the books for young children: *If You Give a Moose a Muffin, If You Give a Mouse a Cookie, If You Give a Pig a Party,* and *If You Take a Mouse to the Movies* by Laura Numeroff. These books take a fun look at consequences and how one decision leads to another.

    Option: Play the country music song "Right or Left at Oak Street" or read the lyrics, available on the Internet as another example of decisions/crossroads and consequences.
2. When women have had a chance to participate, call them together. Remind them that no matter how small we think our decision are, they always have consequences.
3. Share church prayer concerns and ask for additional concerns. Call on the woman you have enlisted to pray.
4. Direct women to their small groups.

Small Group
1. Ask women if they have questions from their study in week 5 and invite them to share points that were significant.
2. Ask women to turn through week 5 and to share Scripture verses that were meaningful to them during their studies of the past week.
3. Write on the board, "Sin is . . ." Ask women to complete that statement. Write their responses on the board.
4. Say: "Kay begins day 1 with, 'Beware of triumph, the confidence of success, its glory, and the entitlements thought to accompany it.' Why this warning? How does it relate to this part of David's life? What does it mean for women today?"
5. In groups of three or four ask women to discuss whether they have been more aware this week of decisions and the short- and long-term consequences of those decisions.
6. With women back together, ask:
    - Why do we usually not think about the consequences of our decisions?
    - How often do we choose not to make decisions but to go act as if on auto-pilot?
7. In pairs, ask women if they have ever had a friend who was a "Nathan" or if they have ever had the courage to be a Nathan to someone else. Remind them that they need not reveal too much personal information.
8. How does society often treat truth tellers? Give an example.
9. Write the word *contrite* on the board. Lead a discussion about being brokenhearted over the awareness of sin in your life.
10. Return to large group for video 6.

Large Group
1. Ask women to turn to the viewing guide for week 6 (p. 118).
2. After the video return to small groups.

Small Group
1. Write on the board the word *Grace*.
2. Ask women in groups of three or four to share a time when someone showed grace to them. It may or may not have anything to do with sin or repentance.
3. Tell women that in this last week of study they will see the power of God's grace in David's life. They can trust God to show the same grace toward them.
4. Encourage women to complete their studies this week and announce that in the last session will discuss their work in week 6 and have a celebration party to enjoy fellowship and God's goodness.
5. Pray, asking God to help these women seek God's forgiveness for any sin in their lives and then to be able to forgive themselves.

Session 7

Before the Session

1. Enlist women to provide finger foods for the celebration.
2. Prepare background Christian music to play when women arrive and during the party.
3. Enlist a woman to pray at the beginning of the large group session.
4. Provide note cards and pens.

During the Session

1. As women arrive, gather in small groups and share a benefit received from the study.
2. When women have arrived and had opportunity to participate, invite them to share a word of praise, encouragement, or hope. List these on the board.
3. Share church prayer concerns and ask for additional concerns. Call on the woman you have enlisted to pray.
4. Direct women to their small groups.
5. Ask women if they have any questions from their study in week 6.
6. Invite women to share points from week 6 that were significant to them.
7. Write the word *discipline* on the board. Invite women to share reasons discipline is needed to help a child. Write these on the board. Then ask, How does God's discipline help His children grow in the right direction?
8. Ask a volunteer to read 2 Samuel 24:24. Ask: Does worship have a price? What does it cost women to worship today?
9. Ask: How does sin impede all forward progress? How does grace empower?
10. Distribute note cards and pens. Ask women to write one decision or promise or commitment they want to make to God as a result of this study. Invite volunteers to share their goals, but do not press all women to share the decisions they have made.
11. Invite women to share reasons to celebrate based on truths from God's Word.
12. Say sentence prayers of thanksgiving and praise. Then enjoy food and fellowship together.

Can a simple conversation
change your life?

It can.

Priscilla Shirer invites you to throw open the doors of communication with God. While you will learn more about God's Word than ever before, the purpose of this first-ever UnBible study is to equip you to hear and respond directly from God. *(6 sessions, plus introduction)* Find out more at www.lifeway.com/women, 1.800.458.2772, or LifeWay Christian Stores.

LifeWay | Women

It's tough
being a woman

Beth Moore's Bible study on Esther provides lessons of faith and courage. Esther, while a queen, was also a foreigner and an orphan. She faced life-and-death decisions. She thwarted an evil plan to destroy her people. And you thought your life was hard! Esther looked to God to deliver her—and she wasn't disappointed. Her destiny can be yours as God sustains you through the challenges of life. *(10 sessions)* Find out more at www.lifeway.com/women, 1.800.458.2772, or LifeWay Christian Stores.

LifeWay | Women

www.lifeway.com/women